1

Back:
Rebirth After Stroke

By Royce Amy Morales

"The worst way to miss a person is to be sitting right beside them, knowing things will never be the same."
— anonymous

"You start preparing for the eventual loss of your partner from the very first day you're together. What you don't prepare for is losing them when they are still alive." - Royce Morales

Foreword

When Michael, my 56 year old husband of 29 years, had a massive, ischemic (blood clot) stroke on November 24, 2014, it didn't take long to realize I was being presented with phenomenal opportunities to practice (and have tested) the spiritual concepts I'd been teaching others for decades.

With nowhere to hide, or a get-out-of-jail-free card.

On day two of his stroke, I spontaneously posted my first message on Facebook. In minutes, I received responses that were encouraging, compassionate, and most importantly, sincerely interested in what we were going through.

At that point I wasn't much of a Facebook activist. Never once considered using it to express my inner (and outer) trials. However, it felt like a virtual hug to have people offering up their caring comments, encouraging me to write more and keep them posted.

So, every night for almost six weeks, I'd sit in the hospital next to my stroked-out-of-it husband, words pouring onto updates. I held nothing back, exposing the depth of my fears along with the daily challenges we faced. And, every post added an important Spiritual Lesson, since that's who I am and how I walk through life.

Followers grew. Friends, family, strangers, people I barely remembered from high school, commented they couldn't wait to hear my "next episode." Each claimed they were personally touched by what I was sharing.

Astonished, I began to see these spontaneous ramblings as the next step in my ongoing purpose as a spiritual teacher. It reaffirmed that the best way to reach others is by sharing personal experiences.

Once Michael came home from the hospital, I stopped posting as often. However, whenever I had the chance, I continued writing, sensing that this experience needed to be in a book format.

Writing became my therapy during surreal times of confusion and fear. It allowed me to focus on this oft-times horrendous experience in Higher Consciousness ways, being in gratitude rather than victimhood.

I hope these raw, heartfelt words coming straight from my experience touch you or someone you love.

– Royce

You've Got to be Kidding

In a deep sleep, I feel my husband poking my leg repeatedly. When I jump awake, Michael has an odd look on his face.

He says in a gravelly voice, a voice I barely recognize: *I feel weird.*

My first response: *Michael, are you messing with me?*

This man is quite the joker. He frequently fools Ms. Gullible (as he calls me) with the same tricks he's repeated dozens of times. It wouldn't be unusual for him to think this is funny.

Without smiling, he assures he's not. His serious expression confirms.

Something inside instantly knows to believe him.

Especially when his words begin to slur and he can't stick out his tongue. In a daze, I somehow I remember I'm supposed to ask him to do that.

Adrenaline starts surging; heart pounding a frantic drum solo. I feel nauseous.

Should I take you to the E.R.? Words I've never considered uttering since we both proudly boast not ascribing to Western Medicine. To say the least.

Without hesitation he nods his head YES.

Right then, I know something must be *really* wrong because his normal response would've been a defiant NO WAY. The next several minutes are a comedy of errors with neither of us laughing. He struggles to get dressed. I help him as best I can. Stunned, I see he's incapable of tying his own shoes.

Trying to blame all of this on panic, but part of me knows this is something else. Something big.

I never imagined could happen to him, a healthy, active, athletic, brilliant man who's been vegetarian for decades. For some reason, I always thought that defied any genetic predisposition from a father with several medical issues.

Convincing him to not worry about brushing his short spikey hair, we frantically race to our car.

With terror clouding logic, I can't remember where the closest hospital is. My hands tremble as I program the GPS. At the first turn I realize it's taking us on an incorrect route.

"Are we going the right way?" I ask Michael, a stereotypic man who prides himself on never losing his sense of direction. He shakes his head and points the opposite way.

I gun it. Thankfully, three-in-the-morning streets are void of traffic, and no cops are lurking in bushes. We arrive at the emergency room in a record five minutes flat, easily park in the almost empty parking structure.

Holding his hand, we wildly scramble the fifty feet from our car toward the brightly lit entrance. Little did I know that was to be his last run.

The waiting room is relatively empty, a few sit slumped over or sleepily watch TV, head in hands. The efficient front desk person asks what's going on, and before I can reply with the only detail I have (*"He said he feels weird"*), the double door flings open and he's just about flung into a wheel chair.

Firing questions as I trot to keep up, his ability to speak rapidly disappears. *Is he diabetic? How is his cholesterol? Does he have hypertension? Does he smoke?*

The word *stroke* is mentioned in hushed tones. I hear it loudly.

Before I even put my purse down, they hook him up to several daunting machines and ask more questions. Now, he's completely unable to answer, so I do my best.

Based on their calm, precise urgency, I'm correct: Something big is happening.

They don't have to repeat the word *stroke*. I know.

Admittedly, I've never thought much when people have told me someone had a stroke. Or when they told me *they* had a stroke. Didn't think it was a big deal. A little paralysis on one side, a little slurred speech... no big deal.

This is a big deal. A Big Deal.

But that doesn't stop denial from slinking in and become my instant best friend. I insist to myself that *this is just a mild episode and he'll be fine in a few hours.*

Sitting at his bedside, the hours tick by. He loses more

and more abilities. My firm grasp on denial starts to slip.
I start admitting that *something serious is happening.*

Transferring him to a bed in the ICU is the final hint.

I watch a continuous blur of gray-faced doctors look at
charts, do more tests and ask a litany of questions. I watch
the man I married almost three decades ago, lay there
drooling, incontinent and not able to comprehend what's
happening.

All I can do is sit by his bed, stroke his face and wonder what
 in the hell to do next.

Denial is sent to the corner to color.

Knowing All

It's almost 7:00 a.m. and he's settling into his ICU bed.
This new wing of the hospital has freshly purchased furniture
so the chair by his side is still relatively comfortable.

The nurses are changing shifts so we sit by ourselves, the
sound of machines attached to him making blipping noises.

It's quiet enough for my thoughts to take over.

Thinking back over the last few weeks. I had a strong
intuitive sense that something was 'off' about Michael.

He'd been extremely edgy, flying off the handle at the tiniest
situation. He was tired (he rarely gets tired), kept getting
headaches (another rarity) and this genius man complained
he couldn't focus. Even on simple things.

When he woke up three days ago with his right eye as red as
a stop sign, my sensing went into full gear. *I knew
something was wrong.*

Big wrong.

But, instead of connecting the dots, we both attributed it to
just stress. Something we're both very used to as retail shop
owners during this end-of-year, pre-holiday craziness.

Now, sitting by his hospital bed, watching several
intimidating machines monitoring vital signs, dots
marching together in unison. My husband officially
becomes another statistic – someone who wasn't taking
proper care of himself.

Or, as I see it, a guilty wife who didn't *insist* that her husband take better care of himself.

The sweet numbness of another layer of denial lifts. Finding a space devoid of electrodes, I gently lay my head on his chest. Tears flow, moistening Michael's hospital gown.

Little did I know how long this trail of tears would be.

This Stroke Thing

The 7:30 a.m. group text I send to our son, family and close friends is simple: *Michael had a stroke and is in the ICU.*

My phone rings immediately. Son calls from London where he's doing business, wanting to know if he should catch the next plane home. I assure him the stroke is mild but will keep him posted.

Part of me wants to cry hysterically and say yes, get here NOW, but I restrain myself. After all, Michael is a healthy, strong, 56 year old and will be fine pretty quick.

Even though it's a stroke.

Completely ignorant about strokes, I think, *what's the big deal? Michael can heal himself of this just like he does with everything else.*

Michael is a phenomenal massage therapist/energy healer who helps people get in touch with physical issues and release them. No matter what ails him or others, he's able to tap into healing energy and manifest miracles.

I'm in total trust that he'll be able to heal this *stroke thing* just as effortlessly.

An hour later I compose another group text, calmly stating that the situation is worse than I thought.

This "mild" stroke is actually quite massive. The doctor examining him calls it *left side ischemic* (a blood clot) which affects all the right side functions as well as speech.

Our son calls again and says he's getting on a plane as soon as he can. I don't argue this time.

Eating My Words

My pride at never needing to see a doctor, putting faith in alternative healing vs. Western Medicine, comes crashing down.

Silently, I thank God for all those things I used to scoff at. Like drugs, medical machinery and a need for someone or something else to heal us.

Trying to stomp out the guilt rearing up for ignoring Michael's blatant clues, I focus on the healthy choices we've always made.

For almost three decades, we've been staunch vegetarians, thinking that's the ultimate way to guarantee perpetual health. A few years ago, Michael was diagnosed as pre-diabetic, but kicked the symptoms by eating even more consciously.

When he was told he had high blood pressure, he immediately started taking a homeopathic remedy, trusting, not verifying, that it worked.

Oh well, joke's on us.

Out of (Remote) Control

After three days in the ICU, with me sleeping on a cot next to him, Michael is transferred to a post-acute care room. Staff is poking and prodding and medicating and telling me what to expect. I listen, but brain fog makes it almost impossible to comprehend their words.

He lays helplessly, unable to move his entire right side, wordless, incapable of swallowing. There's a feeding tube stuffed in a now swollen, red nose, catheter attached to a urine bag, blood pressure automatically taken every hour. Test after test, nurses bustling in, doctors silently reading his chart, bags and drips changing regularly.

Sitting like a numbly next to a man I used to know, I feel lost, confused, terrified, and out of control.

Michael now makes Neanderthal grunts, gesturing, and snapping when he wants something. Most of the time he doesn't even know what he wants or needs.

In the next few days there's slight improvement. I'm grateful for anything signaling progress. Any vital sign that stabilizes, any evidence that my husband is still in there; a little more cognizant, a little less caveman-ish.

Meanwhile, things I never knew happen from a stroke start happening. Like him not understanding even the simplest commands. Not knowing what his body parts are. Not recognizing people he's known his entire life.

Scariest of all: A television addict not even able to work the remote. Down the rabbit hole of hopelessness I go.

Scary Thoughts

A parade of thoughts continue, marching two by two, as I watch my husband lying feebly in a hospital bed.

Thoughts like: *Will I be married to an invalid? Will he be able to continue to work at our store? Will he ever be my "logical half" to balance out my emotional/spiritual side again? Will we be able to have sex again? Who will I be married to? What the hell am I going to do now?*

The one thought I don't want to entertain enters on its own volition: *What if he dies?*

It's heartening to realize he's not suffering, a full-time resident in a stroke-induced Happy Place. Not a care in the world. Kidding around using facial expressions no matter what any of the medical professionals do to him.

Instantly, Michael becomes their favorite patient.

Silently, I make up for it living in my own personal hell.

Inserting the NG Feeding Tube

On day five in the transition unit, his nurse announces he needs to have his NG feeding tube changed. I figure, no big deal since he already has one in. Not the case.

She enters the room with a metal container and a snake-coiled tube wrapped in a plastic bag. The tube looks as long as Michael is tall. Sure doesn't look that long stuffed up his nose.

Nurse arrives filled with attitude. She hasn't dealt with Michael yet, so his attempts at messing with her fall flat.

She takes out the old tube easily enough. Although not a pleasant procedure, it wasn't terrible either. However, the minute she tries to insert the new one, he starts resisting.

I've never seen his face like this before. Anger, rage, confusion, temper-tantrumed child not understanding what's going on. And this man-child doesn't.

With the sudden strength of a prize fighter, he battles the nurse's attempts to insert this thin tube down his nose. The previous tube was inserted when he was so out of it he hadn't tried to fight.

Now he's relentless.

Comfort doesn't work. Logic doesn't work. Holding him down doesn't work.

This petite woman in green scrubs becomes Nurse Ratchet,
sternly threatening him like an irate mother at her wits end.
It doesn't work.

Being treated like a child, he becomes one, hiding his
head under the blanket. Maybe no one will see him there.

"Can't you sedate him a little?" I meekly ask. *(Holy shit, she's
a nurse. Shouldn't she have thought of this?)* Happily,
she agrees, sends in another nurse who adds some
bliss-out medicine in one of his IV's.

It works instantly. Being stoned helps. The tube slides in
like butter.

The Problem with Speaking

Apraxia is when the brain says move but the body won't do it. The message gets confused from the stroked brain's disconnected synapses.

Aphasia is when the words are in there but can't be retrieved. Like a 24/7 Senior Moment.

Michael has both. What a combo.

I remember the excitement at my son's first words. On the tail came the thought: *Oh no, now he's going to start asking for things! And before you know it, he'll be a teenager borrowing my car!*

Michael forms his first post-stroke words: "I want..." but can't form the third part of the sentence to say *what* he wants. I ask him to point, but he shrugs his still shruggable left shoulder and looks confused.

He has no idea why he can't access the words that are sitting in his brain. He has no idea why I can't understand what he's trying to ask for.

What a bundle of confusion and frustration. At least, on my end.

Scared Shitless

It's the middle of the night after an exhausting, frustrating day starting various therapies. Michael's asleep in his hospital bed and I'm sleeping on the world's most uncomfortable (but who's complaining) cot three feet away.

Snapping his fingers, as he's figured out how to do, I jump out of a rare deep sleep and go to his side.

"What's wrong? What do you want? Are you okay?"

He repeats a few indecipherable words sounding like cave man grunts. "I'm so sorry, Michael, I just don't understand what you're trying to say," I repeat.

Frustration mounts in both of us. His face turns into a grimace and he starts crying. A cry I've never heard from him. Like a lost and terrified child.

The man I know better than any human on the planet cannot get me to understand what he wants to say.

Stopping for a second, I remember that one of the things we've always done with each other is to freely acknowledge our fears. Without judgement or trying to fix, just to release them.

Suddenly I understand.

I look directly in his eyes and ask, "Are you afraid?"

He nods his head gratefully. His strong left hand holds mine with a death grip. Cupping his face, I try to comfort. But what can I say? How can I help with fears I share as my own?

Our tears merge as I tell him I'm afraid too. Scared shitless, actually.

In the dim light, I stare at the man I married, a man with tubes sticking out from far too many orifices. Another protective layer of the veil of denial lifts. The intensity of what we're going through hits.

Like several tons of bricks.

It's all about guilt.

Without saying a word, he knows something's surfacing in me. His furrowed brow says "What's wrong?"

Immediately, my crying intensifies.

Big messy sobs with no concern for how noisy I'm being.

Bending over him, I hold tightly to his shoulders, one of the few places without any foreign objects inserted.

Without holding back, guilt overflows and I start apologizing for everything.

"I should've seen this coming," I stammer. "I knew something was wrong with you for weeks, but I kept justifying it, saying it was just stress."
Apologies fly out, as messily as my tears.

"I should've been stricter with you and made sure you monitored your blood pressure and sugar level. I should've made sure! I'm so sorry, Michael, so so sorry."

As I've trained him to do, he just listens, expertly hearing what I'm expressing, allowing me time and space to go through it (so much easier since he can't talk).

After I purge, he hugs me tight with his strong left arm, stroking my hair.

After several minutes, I pull away from his hold. He gives Me a look that says *it's okay*, and we hold each other some more.

"I want you back. I want you back. Michael, I know you're in there. I want you back." More tears.

As always, just listening to expressed fears allows them to flitter away, back to wherever acknowledged fears go.

Even with a stroke patient.

Crawling back to "bed," I have lucid, nightmarish dreams, about storm troopers getting him. *Gotta save him. Gotta hide him.*

I know I can't.

Ten Thousand Years of Karma

Tonight, as I do one more thing for Michael, he politely says *thank you.*

Jokingly, I reply: "You'll get a bill!"

He smiles.

I believe that at the end of each life, we do a tally as to how much we gave and how much we took to see if we balanced out our Give/Receive Balance Sheet of Life.

That's how I see karma. Did we *fully give love, unconditionally,* and did we *allow ourselves to be loved, unconditionally,* as much as we set out to?

That is the True Meaning of why we are here, our Purpose, whether we know it or not.

I've been teaching classes on spiritual awakening and personal development for over three decades. I teach how to discover why certain things keep occurring, stuck patterns that just won't resolve.

These patterns may appear to be from things experienced in this life, but I find that they always source back to previous lifetimes.

Lives we've become amnesiac to, but their subconscious influence still affect us. Especially from traumatic events.

Teaching others allows just as much inner work for me. And, since Michael used to be one of my students, he's just as committed to the work as well.

When I first started teaching in the late '70's, I had a student who was very involved in Transcendental Meditation (T.M.) movement. He had gone on a two week advanced program where they were teaching how to levitate (or "fly," as they termed it).

He explained that the group of about a hundred seekers sat on cushions in a big open warehouse, all in full lotus position. They would go into a deep, meditative state with the intention to lift up from their seats.

At first, he explained, it was more like hopping, bouncing, strongly willing the body to rise. As he tried to perform this fete, he hop-landed on his tailbone and actually broke it.

Painfully.

Maharishi (the founder of T.M.) just happened to be there that week and got wind of what happened to this man. He approached him and said, in typical mystical guru fashion: "Ahhh, that is ten thousand years of karma you just cleaned up!"

Apparently, if you injure yourself while attempting to do something spiritually based, you're awarded a Get Out Of Karma Free Card. Or something like that.

Decades later, talking to my stroked husband, this story came back to me.

How much karma am I paying off going through this with Michael?

I decide to broach the subject.

"Michael, I think this whole stroke thing is about really cleaning things up, our karma, and not needing to suffer any more."

He's lying in bed, looking at me with comprehension in his eyes, minus the ability to add to the conversation.

"Remember how we've gotten in touch with why there are always so many struggles in this life for us?"

He nods his head.

During several meditations, we both remembered past lives being together. There were a variety of roles we'd chosen, yet all had similar themes: Suffering, pain, death.

We also remembered being in a between lives realm where we agreed to complete that cycle by cleaning up what we'd done in those past incarnations. So we wouldn't need to repeat the struggle in our next life, this one.

"I'm feeling like your stroke was the grand crescendo, cleaning up something huge."

He nods yes, eyes downcast, pondering my words.

"But, did you really need to go to such extremes to do that?" I ask, snarkily.

A slight smile from the strong side of his droopy mouth answers my question.

I kiss his forehead. I think this time we finally accomplished it.

I hope so.

Thank God he's in there, understanding what I say, even when it's pretty "out there" like I am.

Off to the Ranch

After posting another Michael Update on Facebook, one of our friends messages to see if I'd heard of Rancho Los Amigos Rehab Hospital. Being new to all this, I reply that I've never heard of it.

He explains that it's the number one place in the U.S. for stroke rehab, and that I should get him in there asap. He offers to help since he has "good connections."

Of course I take him up on his offer, and, within days, to the utter shock the entire hospital staff, Michael is accepted there. Later I discover that this is quite a miraculous feat since Rancho has a seriously long waiting list.

Amazing.

It's the middle of December, almost ten at night, pouring rain, when the ambulance arrives to transport him to Rancho. Loading him on a gurney, I kiss him good bye, and watch as they drive off.

I have no idea how to get to Rancho. GPS set, blinded by rain, fear and tears, I head out. An hour later, I'm traversing streets I've never been on, in a city I've heard of but never seen.

Somehow, eventually I land in the sprawling parking lot. There's no signage as to where to go, so I start frantically asking people who seem to know where they're going.

Starting to panic, I envision my husband lying helplessly on a stretcher, not able to talk, brought somewhere in this maze of a hospital, without me ever finding him.

Going into yet one more building, the front desk person tells me where he *might* be (no record of an incoming patient yet). "Go that way," she points, "and keep walking toward the right. He's probably in the JPI building."

What the heck is a JPI building?

Somehow I figure out that JPI stands for Jacqueline Perry Institute (written on a roof sign barely seen by glasses blurred with rain). Once inside, the guard directs me to go to the second floor where he "probably" is. Still no admissions list.

Longest corridor of my life. Tears streaming, I stop at the nurse's station. Reading a book, she looks up, not an iota of compassion in her bored, expressionless face.

"I'm trying to find my husband and the guard told me to try here," my voice cracking. I'm about to lose it.

"Oh, yes, I think we had a new patient just brought in by ambulance. Let me check..."

She confirms that it's Michael, telling me he's right across the hall in room 272. I rush in and there he is, comfy, cozy in bed, grinning with the TV on already.

Grabbing his shoulders, I hold on like I haven't seen him in years.

A young nurse wearing Snoopy scrubs walks in and introduces herself. "Hi, my name is Joann. Are you his wife?"

Still shaky, I describe what I just went through.

Compassionately, she apologizes. Reaching out, she gives me a warm, welcoming hug. Exactly what I need right now.

Taking me down the hall into a tiny, desk-filled room, she asks a bunch of questions, filling out form after form. When we're done, I ask one of my own: *Can I sleep in the room here with Michael?*

I haven't left his side since rushing to the hospital almost two weeks ago. Can't imagine leaving him here by himself.

"Of course!" she says, and proceeds to wheel in an actual fold up bed for me to sleep on. Anything's better than the chair contraption I've been using at the other hospital.

Thanking her for her kindness, still tearful, I return her recent hug.

Without knowing how rehab works, I'm just thrilled to know he will be getting the best care. Figuring they'll fix him up quick and we'll head home.

Again, clueless.

First Day at Rancho

Although Michael has no problem sleeping wherever he lands, my first night at Rancho is anything but restful. The bed is lumpy; the hall is bustling with staff coming in every few hours to check his blood pressure, rudely awakening me each time.

And we have a roommate.

Although a curtain separates the room, just knowing we aren't alone makes me uncomfortable and self-conscious.

It's morning and several nurses arrive. Testing begins. Questions, instructions, scheduling. By the time breakfast appears, I'm overwhelmed with what "rehab" actually entails.

Having not eaten since breakfast the day before, I ask one of the nurses where I can purchase food. She looks at me strangely and says there's a cafeteria through the parking lot. Or there's a cart downstairs.

Recalling my adventure in the parking lot last night, I opt for the cart, bringing a very unhealthy muffin back to the room.

As soon as I sit down, several people walk in, introducing themselves as Michael's team of therapists. Physical Therapy, Occupational Therapy, Speech Therapy, Recreational Therapy and a few student interns by their sides.

They explain his schedule which consists of six hours of structured therapy every day except Sunday.

"All of the therapy we do is about waking up his muscles, getting synapses in his brain to create new pathways," one of the therapists explains.

I'm thrilled he's going to receive so much care, anticipating that, with all this focused treatment, he will be fine in a couple of weeks.

"Am I allowed to accompany him into therapy?" I ask.

"Absolutely! You'll need to learn all this so you can be a better caregiver," they explain.

Caregiver?

Another new concept I never imagined, figuring we'd go back to running our shop and nothing would change.

Like a facial masque long overdue to be removed, more denial peels away.

Let the Therapy Begin!

Head spinning as Michael's "team" exits, I sit on my bed watching TV in a daze. *What the fuck?*

His new Speech Therapist returns to our room at 10:15, apologizing for being late. "Just so you know, I'm always late," she says with a non-apologetic grin.

Instantly, I'm comfortable with this somewhat sarcastic professional.

She immediately begins talking to Michael directly. Maybe she doesn't realize he can't talk? I try to answer for him, but she ignores me, directing everything right to him. As though he will suddenly be able to reply. Maybe she hasn't read his chart?

I look on with a blend of amazement and melancholy, wondering if my husband's words will ever return.

Abruptly she says "Okay, let's go to my office and start therapy."

As I watch, she gets him out of bed and straps him into a wheelchair lickety split. Off they go.

Half running to keep up, she at last engages me in conversation.

"When was his stroke? How old is he? What hospital was he transferred from? Has he made any improvement?"

Answering as rapid fire as each question is thrown, we arrive at her office. It's small, with two L-shaped desks butting next to each other. Inspirational quotes hang on every wall; meaningful message cards grace the desks; a bulletin board is pinned with spiritual sayings. Good to know we speak the same language.

"Okay, Michael, my name is Randy and I'm your speech therapist. What's your name?" she asks, slowly and clearly, over-emphasizing the pronunciation of each word.

I hold back answering for him as he struggles to even remember his name. She figures out he's not going to say it so she gives him the first sound.

"Mmmmmm...." she says, expanding long on the em sound. She motions for him to finish the word.

He doesn't.

She says "Michael" several times, accentuating the words with her mouth and pointing to is so he can mimic.

He doesn't.

For an instant her eyes catch mine. Certain she sees my tears welling, but continues working with Michael.

He starts getting goofy, his best thing, and she plays along with him.

She asks several simple yes/no questions, and the majority of times his answers are wrong.

"Are you at Disneyland?" "Yes!" "Are you sure you mean yes?" she asks and he shakes his head emphatically.

She asks him where the window is and he looks at her blankly. He has no idea what she's asking or what a window is.

She asks him to say the alphabet with her. A few garbled letters are spoken out of order.

She points at a calendar. "Can you show me what date it is?" Clueless.

"Okay," she says, acknowledging even the little bit he was able to do.

She directs the rest of the session to me, asking more questions about Michael, reiterating what I'd already been told about Aphasia and Apraxia.

"Aphasia means the inability to retrieve words and it's really common after a stroke. Although many people have never heard of it, over a million Americans have it. Recovery can take months, if not years, and there are usually long term deficits." More details to add to my mush brain that doesn't want to understand.

"I see he has a feeding tube," she says with a look of disgust. "How long has it been in?"

"Well, they recently changed it a few days before we transferred here. It was a terrible ordeal for him. I'm not a professional, but it sure seems to me that part of his swallowing problem is that feeding tube in the way. Does that make sense?"

"Well, yes, it does. There are lots of conflicting opinions about NG tubes. But, we'll start focusing on getting his ability
to swallow back so he can have it taken out," she explains.

"Just so you know, I have a lot of success retraining stroke victims to remember how to swallow. It just takes time, and he has another week or so before it has to be changed again. We'll start tomorrow in your room. I'll bring some thickened water and see what I can do."

Thickened water sounds about as palatable as most hospital food, but if it can help Michael re-learn to swallow, I'm all for it.
She wheels him back to his room. I thank her profusely

Even before the tears can start, his Physical Therapist arrives and off we go again. I love it here already.

You Don't Really Know Someone Until You See an X-ray of Them Swallowing.

After twelve days at his other hospital, Michael still isn't able to swallow. His second day at Rancho, his speech therapist decides to do a video x-ray while feeding him spoons of apple sauce laden with glowing barium.

I get to watch.

It takes three conscious efforts to get a spoonful down, but he manages. They're concerned about aspiration, wanting him to be better at swallowing before they permanently remove the NG tube.

We head back to our room. Within minutes, four white-coated, official looking doctors march in.

"We are here to talk to you about inserting a G-Tube," one says with doctor-like authority.

They explain that a G-tube is a feeding method that's inserted directly into the stomach. They start rattling off the importance of doing this, and what a simple procedure it is. No Big Deal, they all emphasize.

Every meeting we've had with his speech therapist, she's focused on getting him to swallow so they won't have to insert a G-tube. I've never asked why she's opposed to one, but I can tell by her attitude that it's something we *do not want*.

The doctors proceed to tell me that his NG tube needs to be removed soon since it's been in over two weeks. I ask if we can wait a few more days since he's making such good progress with his swallowing therapy.

"Okay," one says grudgingly. "We'll wait until the end of his therapy session tomorrow because the doctor that does the procedure is going out of town and it needs to happen!"

Feeling backed in a corner, meekly I agree.

How do I know what to do? What do I know about G-tubes and making sure my helpless husband gets fed?

The white-coats leave and minutes later, his speech therapist walks in. Upset, I start telling her what just happened with the army of doctors. Quickly, she hushes me.

"Let's talk in my office," she says, looking around to make sure no one overheard.

Taking quick strides down the hall, we reach her tiny treatment room. She sits me down and proceeds to explain her feelings about G-Tubes. Prefacing everything with "I don't mean to say anything against what the doctors recommend, but...."

Reading between the lines, I discern her meaning.

She proceeds to work with Michael on swallowing for almost two hours. A lot of progress has been made even since yesterday.

Getting up to leave her office, she casually asks what I've decided to do. "I know in my gut that he will be able to swallow and I just don't feel good about inserting a tube in his stomach," I say with new-found confidence.

Apparently Michael's been listening intently to our conversation. He grabs my hand, looks frantic and struggles to get a sentence out. It's mostly garbled, but the therapist and I clearly hear what he's trying to express: NO TUMMY TUBE!

It's the final sign I need assuring that my decision is the right one.

In my daily Facebook update, I share about this difficult decision saying no to a G-Tube. Within minutes, I receive a personal message from a friend who happens to be a health-care manager: "Good choice! G-Tubes are bad news. Very painful and prone to infection!"

One more confirmation.

Just a Spoonful of Apple Juice Helps the Medicine Go Down

To help re-train his slow esophagus, the speech therapist suggests that electrode stimulation (E-Stim) will help. I'm willing to try anything to avoid the dreaded G-Tube.

The first step to accomplish this, she explains, is to shave off a lot of his beard so that the pads with current can reach him.

I've never shaved a man before.

Trying to be gentle, I scrape and scrape. He flinches in pain. There's nothing I want to do less than cause him more pain, so I try substituting liquid soap for shaving cream.

It helps a bit, but he's getting antsy. Hoping he's clean shaven enough for tomorrow, I give up.

The next day I explain to my alert but still confused husband: "Your speech therapist is going to put some electric stimulation on your throat today to help you re-learn to swallow." He seems to understand, but it's hard to tell.

All I care about is trying this new tactic.

Randy takes us into her office and attaches four sticky pads under his freshly shaved chin. Turning it on, she asks if the current is painful. He shakes his head no.

She cranks it up until he winces. She stops there. "Okay, so now we're going to give you a spoon full of

apple juice," she explains. His face brightens with the notion
of having anything other than sustenance arriving via his NG. tube.

She puts the spoon in his mouth. It takes four strong swallows, even with electronic stimulation, to get this bit of juice to go down.

As he struggles with this simple, formerly instinctive task, the therapist verbally coaches step by step how to accomplish it. "Close your mouth. Put your tongue on the roof of your mouth and push back," she says, demonstrating with her mouth open so he can see.

As he re-learns this automatic function, I find myself being conscious of my own swallowing mechanism. Never considered how complex it is to just ingest a spoon of juice. How absolutely magical that we do this without thought. Bodies are amazing.

Sadly, he doesn't pass the test.

Randy assures that he will be able to do it soon. I hear: *You made the right decision to not get a tummy tube.*

The next day she comes into our room with a jar of baby food applesauce in her hand. She opens it, and within seconds, he devours the entire jar! *Without* choking!

I don't know this for a fact, but I would bet she immediately went to the doctor wanting to insert the G-tube to gloat in her success. However, just in case, the NG tube stays in.

Can't wait for that friggin' thing to be removed.

My intuition (and logic) says that the tube is what's preventing him from swallowing easily. How could a long tube forced down one's throat not be getting in the way?

But, what do I know? I do know I made the right decision to not insert a G-Tube.

Cutting the Cord

Feeling pretty shaken after all our adventures these last few days. Starting to reluctantly accept what so many have said in different ways: *Recovery is a long road.*

Trying to stay in the moment, but pessimism starts sneaking its way in. Right past where denial is hiding out.

Michael's speech therapist arrives promptly at 9:00 a.m. with another two jars of baby food in tow. "Okay, let's go outside," she says perkily.

As we start down the hall, we're met by a nurse informing us that they are going to take out his NG tube.

"Oh good! When?" I ask.

"Right now!" she answers.

Randy is elated but tries to remain professional, containing her excitement.

We wheel back to our room, nurse following. With one yank, out it comes, a lot easier than when it was inserted. His nose is sore and swollen, but he immediately perks up and looks like himself again.

Nurse exits. Randy and I are In tears. We all hug.

We head downstairs, rolling out to a round metal table underneath the wide spread of a magnolia tree. She opens the baby food and he grabs it out of her hand. Spoonful by spoonful he devours it. Again, without choking.

She explains that he will need to only eat pureed food for a while, and she will work with him to get ready for real food. I hug her and tell her she is truly an angel.

When his first tray of hospital food arrives at noon, there are four small containers of pureed items. Slightly different colors, they all look the same.

Grabbing them like a starving man, he waves away a spoon, refuses my help, and chugs them. Without choking.

I find his speech therapist and inform her of his success. She's beams, elated. We hug again.

Walking by one of the doctors who had been pushing for the G-tube, I let her know that my husband just ate all his pureed lunch without choking. She half smiles and says *that's great*. I try not to smirk, but I'm sure it leaks out. Just a little.

Spooning, or, Little Things We Take For Granted

I would give anything to be able to snuggle with my husband, either the pre-stroke man or the one he is now. To crawl into the tiny hospital bed and feel his body next to mine. To have him hold me and tell me everything's going to be alright.

In separate beds, we pass out early tonight. As we seem to do every night, we wake up simultaneously at precisely 3:00 a.m. Our eyes meet in the subdued darkness, and, unexpectedly
I'm hit with a serious, unforeseen melt down.

What the fuck am I going to do? What the fuck am I supposed to do? Tell me Universe! Tell me now!

Scary to realize how reliant I've become on this man.

He's the logic to my emotional; the sensible to my spontaneous. As a massage therapist, he's focused on physical issues, whereas my focus is on the spiritual. He's the story teller to my need for bottom line. He's the keeper of details, facts, current events and trivia to my concern with the Big Picture.

He's the editor to my longwinded writings.

We are two balanced puzzle pieces that fit. Really well. Even with some Big Lessons we continue to learn from each other. *I want my husband back.* Tears flowing in the darkness are met by silence.

Away

After breakfast today, I decide to leave the hospital, the first time in weeks. I desperately need a shower and some fresh clothes. It's reminiscent of the first time I left my six month old baby with my mother. Over three decades ago.

Terrifying yet needed.

How can I leave Michael without being his voice? What if he wants something and the nurse isn't there? He can't even use   the call button.

As I'm getting ready to go, I explain that I need to go home, change clothes, take a shower. He nods his head, but I'm not certain he understands.

I inform the nurses desk and she offers a blasé' nod, barely looking up. "Can you let his nurse know I'll be gone about two hours? He's unable to use the call button and he can't talk,"   I explain to this indifferent human.

Rush home, fast shower, fresh clothes, pack a bag of necessities like underwear and socks. Rush back. Gone almost two hours,   I rush into his room anticipating some sort of disaster. All is fine.   He's fine. I can breathe.

Apologizing profusely, I explain *again* why I left.

"Michael, I needed to go home and take a shower and get clean clothes. Did you miss me?"

Obeying the tone of my question, perplexedly he nods his head yes. Not even sure he knew I was gone.

Honestly, I just needed to be away from the hospital and get my wits about me. I hold him and cry. Again.

He looks at me like I'm nuts and says without words, *it's okay,*
I understand.

Glad to be back, I sit next to his bed and clasp his hand.

The entire rest of the day.

Alive and Kicken'

We've been at Rancho a little over a week. Michael has had therapy almost six hours a day and is making slow progress.

PT decides to try something different today.

"Let's put some electrodes on his leg and see if he responds. Sometimes you just have to kick start the muscles again and pathways open up to the brain a bit."

Sure, go for it, I say without hesitation. What the heck.

Two therapists help lay him down on the mat table (a ten by ten, padded, raisable device) and attach electrodes to several places on his leg. I watch in amazement as his muscles jump and dance as the therapist pushes buttons.

Then, miracle upon miracle, PT stops pushing the buttons and the leg continues to move. On its own volition.

"Legs are easier to rehabilitate than arms," he explains.

Why?

"Because the human body needs legs more than it needs arms. We can get along with only one arm, but the mind says we can't walk without two legs, so it connects faster to that motor skill. The memory comes back faster. Makes sense in a rather primitive sort of way."

Yes, makes sense. Bodies are, after all, just primitive mechanisms being stimulated and responding. Thanks Pavlov.

Ah, It's the Little Things

Occupational therapy starts re-teaching Michael how to get dressed. It's far more complicated than most appreciate.

She explains: "Always put your weak arm in first and then slip the shirt over your head and get your strong arm in." Makes sense in a backwards sort of way.

He looks totally confused, clearly doesn't understand. She repeats, this time taking his hand and showing him.

That helps, but he's still zombie-like and I'm not sure what he's able to take in.

At least one of us is getting the lesson. Just remember, *weak arm first*, I say to myself.

We did have one small success: Michael put on his socks with one hand. Just like his dad, who lost an arm in the war, used to do.

I'm learning that an OT is who focuses on arm movement as well as the everyday tasks of living. Like showering, toileting, grooming.

Things us "two hand-ers" take for granted.

Never again.

Bedside Manner?

When the main doctor finally comes in to see Michael after several days of rehab, I'm sitting in a cloud of positive, hopeful energy. After all, the therapists keep telling me how wonderfully he's doing, and I'm seeing constant progress as well.

Albeit baby steps.

So, when this white-coated stranger says, without hesitation or mincing words that *one third of your husband's brain is dead,* the reality hits hard.

Holding back tears, I ask what some may think is obvious: *Will it come back to life?*

Another unminced answer: "No. But the brain is very plastic, and can compensate. The other areas that are not dead will take over and allow him to re-learn and adjust. It will create new pathways. He may not ever be the same, but he could be."

Next obvious question: *How long?*

"Within the first six months we'll know how much progress he'll make, although some people continue to improve up to a year after a stroke, but slowly."

I try hard not to "buy into" this man's "learned" opinion, keeping in mind it IS just an opinion. However, I feel every cell of my body buy it, hook line and sinker. Sinking is more like it.

A Watched Penis Never Pees

After lunch, Michael indicates frantically that he has to pee. I grab the urinal and gently guide his penis in it. Propped up in the hospital bed, he waits and waits. And waits some more.

Occasionally, he takes off the urinal, a minute later grabs it and waits again.

Forty five minutes later, still not a drop.

A helpful nurse tries turning on water. Lovingly, I croon Moon River and ask him to imagine waterfalls. In his goofy adorable way, he looks at Mr. Penis and coos to it like a baby.

Nothing works.

The more we watch expectantly, the more his pee has a mind of its own.

A social worker comes in to talk with me. I turn my back on Michael for two minutes and immediately there's pee everywhere. I call for the nurse to come back in. When she sees the mess we both start laughing until we cry.

Who knew that even the ability to urinate gets affected by a stroke? I guess penises always have a mind of their own, right?

Singin' in the Rain

Yesterday, Michael felt as though he had to pee urgently and nothing happened. Today is the complete opposite. When he   has to go, he *really* has to go.

Sitting in his wheelchair waiting for his PT session, he motions that he *really* has to go. He starts whining and the whines   quickly turn into moans.

Since I am unable to transfer him from his wheelchair to the toilet, I push the nurse call button. No answer. I run to the nurse's station. No one is around.

"Do you have to poop too?" I ask frantically? "Yes!" he nods.

PT arrives just in the nick of time. She runs to get a nurse, and, between the three of us, we get him into the bathroom, pull down his shorts and open the diaper he's still required to wear.

They leave the bathroom for privacy, and, as I lean over to get   the diaper out of the way, he lets loose a stream of pee that reaches across the room!

I dart out of the way, but not quite fast enough to avoid being showered. My boots are soaked. Didn't know they were waterproof until now!

People are into 'golden showers' why?

Two hours later, while lying in bed, he indicates he has to pee.   He reaches for the urinal, loses it under the sheets, and before I can grab it, he's spraying everywhere. The bed, the curtains, his hands.

Grabbing the urinal, I put it over his wildly peeing penis, capturing at least some of it. I run to get the nurse and by the time I return, he dumped what was caught all over the floor.

Even though it's as ridiculous as getting angry at a baby learning to control newly awakening bodily functions, I snap.

"Why did you do that?" I ask in an annoyed mother tone.

Immediately he realizes what did and becomes the sorrowful two year old with a pouty lip.

Immediately I realize what I've done and apologize profusely.

"I'm so sorry Michael. I just thought you knew better, but I guess right now you don't. It's okay," I comfort my sweet baby man.

Pouty lip goes away. Nurse cleans up pee.

Realizing I have a two year old to take care of now.

The Pee of Success

You know you've been doing this stroke stuff too long when you get jubilant that your husband just managed to pee in the urinal.

And not fling it across the room.

So thrilled that you elatedly run up the hall to show the front desk nurse.

She smiles, knowingly. Probably more thrilled to not have to change his sheets yet again.

Call Me By My Name

Since so much time has been spent trying to get Michael to swallow without choking, speech therapy was bumped to the bottom of the list.

Until today.

True to her lateness warning, Randy arrives at 9:20. The three of us roll over to her office.

Taking out a white board, she starts writing down words with an almost dry green marker: Months, years, days of the week.

She asks Michael which is the correct one. He gets every single one right, even the correct day of the week and year. I didn't even know that one since time has no meaning in a hospital.

She then takes out a pack of cards with photos of various objects on them. Laying out three at a time, she asks him to point to the one she's naming.

Out of thirty cards, he gets twenty eight correct.

Odd, the two he missed are hammer and screw driver, tools he used almost every day at our shop.

The brain is a very strange creature indeed.

She then writes down three names and asks which is his. Immediately, he recognizes his name. However, he still stubbornly insists we are in Disneyland and not a hospital.

Wishful thinking? His permanently warped humor?
I ask her to write down three more names to see if he knows
which is mine. He instantly does, even though she wrote
Joyce for one of them as a test.

Life is good.

Maybe because I threaten that, after almost three decades
of marriage, he better get this one right.

Plus, Joyce is the name I give myself when referring to my
evil alter-ego!

Stripped to the Core Intimacy

Standing next to him stretched out on a gurney, we await the latest round of doctor-ordered x-rays.

Out of the blue, every cell in my body vibrates. I'm overcome with love for this man.

Looking at Michael, I'm able to see who he really is, stripped of pretenses, no acts, no need for approval. A helpless, loving baby, with primal needs, simply concerned with survival.

All I feel is love. I. Just. Love. Him.

How can this moment feel more intimate than anything I've ever experienced in our marriage? I hold his hand, stroke his forehead, kiss his cheek – nothing is more intimate.

At this moment, there's nothing more that I need.

The energy in my heart chakra feels like it's been cracked wide open. Adrenalin rushes in; I feel like I'm soaring out of my body. Looking around at the other bodies lying on gurneys, I feel the same intense love for each of them.

Compassion born of empathy. All of us suffering the same pain. Not just those who've ended up here, but for the strength and small triumphs of enduring this scary thing called Life.

Being human.

We are all in the rehab hospital of life.

As a spiritual teacher, I talk in depth about unconditional love with my students. I've felt it frequently, but this is more profound than anything I've yet to feel. Not conceptual, real.

Authentically real.

Thank. Full.

I'd Rather Do it Myself!

It takes an eternity for Michael to get even one simple word out. If he ever does. A two word sentence can take even longer. Usually never happens.

Granted, I have the patience of a saint, but now he doesn't. He gets frustrated, frequently saying, clearly I might add: "I can't do this!" or "I can't think."

It's heartbreaking. The words are churning in his head, but he just can't access them to get them out. Or, *retrieve the words,* as his therapists explain.

It's like that arcade game with the claw that drops and never grabs what you're aiming for. How many quarters can you possibly lose until you give up?

Ahhh, aphasia.

Ever since his feeding tube was removed, he stubbornly wants to do everything himself. Which is a good thing, but often has either messy or dangerous consequences.

He pushes my hand away when trying to open a container for him that takes two hands to accomplish. He waves me off when I offer to help put his shirt on. He says emphatically, "I know!" when I try to explain something.

He's one stubborn man, and that's a good quality to still have.

Sometimes.

Believe me, there's nothing I'd rather have than his independence, but there are some actual limitations.

It's a duality: Wanting to empower him to do it himself, yet knowing what he's now incapable of.

I teach others the importance of not rescuing, how disempowering that can be. And that often times, our need to rescue others, comes from wanting to be rescued ourselves.

Or subconsciously needing recognition, control or pity.

But would a parent allow a child to get so frustrated that they just give up, or would they step in to help in some way?

Intent is the key. Assist from trying to empower, not create dependency or take away trust in self, is where we need to come from.

I trust I will know (and come from) the difference.

Transferring

His physical therapist informs us that she's going to teach me how to do a 'transfer' today.

Repeatedly, I've heard that "rehab-speak" when nurses and therapists help Michael out of bed or off the toilet onto his wheelchair.

All I can say is: *It sure looks easy when they do it.*

Sure glad I've been going to the gym committedly these last three years!

Even before I realize it, PT recognizes my stressed-out brain is mush. She takes out a thick, black Sharpie and writes a ten step instruction sheet in large, bold letters, easy words, so I can follow along. She Xeroxes several copies and posts them all over his room.

Especially in the bathroom.

It's embarrassing how frustrating this simple action is for me. You never know how frazzled you are until, things that should be simple, are completely overwhelming and just won't click.

Like Michael, lately I can barely remember my *own* name.

Reading the lists aloud, repeatedly, I check off everything I'm supposed to do as I do it. Nothing gets past the impenetrable brain soup.

Michael listens as hard as he can but, like me, none of it's registering.

Every time we practice, I remind him (me) to scoot his butt forward in the chair to get standing leverage. I remind him (me) to use a grab bar to pull up from. I remind him (me) to angle the wheels just right, toward his weak side, and to always make sure the brakes are on. That one I somehow remember.

Amazing the things I've never noticed when performing the simple action of getting up from a chair.

After dozens of tries, finally, it clicks. Really clicks! Wow, it's   so friggin easy! Why couldn't I get this before?

Isn't that how everything is in life?

Learning to drive seemed overwhelmingly impossible; now it happens without thought. Working on a computer, at first, seemed incomprehensible and confusing; now it's second nature.

Taking care of a wheelchair bound husband: Soon to be a piece   of cake.

Stress power.

Mr. Finicky

The new Michael is suddenly obsessively compulsive about everything.

If there's a piece of paper hung on the wall, he relentlessly points at it until I tell him what it says. If an object is moved in his space, it upsets him. If he needs to be cleaned up, he gets irritated until it happens, immediately.

Not like the Mr. Messy I used to be married to.

Must give him some sense of control in his out-of-control world I guess.

Ready or Not? Not!

Today Michael gets to do some balancing/strengthening exercises in a "standing box," a contraption that completely supports the patient, relieving fear of falling backwards.

Or forwards. Or sideways.

On the way back to our room, a PT runs down the hall after us. She explains that a psychologist is giving a presentation called "Life After Stroke," and recommends that we attend.

What the heck. All we have is time here.

The presenter talks about the anticipated stages of emotions post stroke, borrowed from Elizabeth Kubler-Ross's *Stages of Grief:* Denial, bargaining, anger, guilt, sadness, repeat.

It all makes sense.

Problem is, strokes are like having a person die but still be alive.

After only a couple of weeks, I've done all the stages. Repeat.

Afterwards, we're apprehended by his main physical therapist and told to follow. Obediently, we do, only to find his entire   team of therapists, plus a case worker and social worker, stone faced, waiting in a small room.

Not knowing what's going on, my expression shifts to terror as I stand in front of what looks like The Inquisition.

Since I wear emotions on my sleeve, a therapist quickly assures me that this is just a 'team meeting' to talk about Michael's progress. No need to panic.

After informing me that he's doing really well, they let me know that his estimated release date is December 24th.

My stomach double flips.

Not only is that the busiest day of the year at my shop (although I haven't been there in weeks), it seems WAY TOO SOON!

The color drains from my already make-up free face. Several therapists ask if I'm okay, and do I have any questions.

"Well, no, but that seems awfully soon. Is there any room for negotiation about that?" I ask, panic rising rapidly.

"Well, we will be able to re-assess as we get closer to that date," one PT assures in her best formal voice.

After the meeting, I wheel Michael out of the conference room, head over to the dining room where a chorale group visiting from the L.A. Opera is caroling. The minute I hear one note, sobbing starts. Yet again.

Uncontrollably.

The holiday music touches me in ways it used to prior to owning my shop, being forced to hear Christmas music 25 days straight. For 21 years.

Standing behind Michael's wheelchair, leaning on the handles to hold me upright, my tears dampen the top of his head. The reality of his homecoming is terrifying. The reality of who he is now is terrifying.

The reality of what the fuck am I going to do is terrifying.

Being safe in the womb of his rehab hospital can't be going away this soon. *I'm not ready!*

Michael belts out Christmas songs, some accurate words, some Neanderthal, all the way back to our room.

He's oblivious to the tear-drenched top of his head.

A Stroke is not a Strike out!

The next day, Michael's speech therapist informs him that he's going to sing to her. I think, *oh no, that will never work.*

Who knew that no matter how massive a stroke, some things are recorded forever on the brain's hard drive. Seems there's a little memory chip containing one's own personal play list on the right side of the brain. The creative side, the part that wasn't impacted by his stroke.

Now, under pre-stroke circumstances, his response would've been "No way, I don't sing!" Unless, of course, he's in the car with the radio on full blast and windows up. 60's rock is his genre of choice. Nothing else.

Without giving him an inch to refuse, she explains that he's going to sing "Take Me Out to the Ballgame." Baseball fanatic that he is, his immediate reaction is an excited head bob, clearly saying YES!

To start him off, she shamelessly belts it out at the top of her lungs.

Seconds later, he happily starts singing along! Granted, most of the words are garbled, but the rhythm and phrasing is perfect. Holding up one, two, three fingers, he strikes out that other team!

And, the clearest word he pronounces is, you guessed it, DODGERS, exactly when it's time to insert one's favorite team.

I'm mesmerized, watching a man whose entire vocabulary consists of "I want____," "abadaba," an occasional grunt and twice saying "I love you," gleefully singing as if he's in the seventh inning stretch. (Or is it the sixth inning? I don't know, I'm usually bored out of my mind by then.)

We both cheer and high-five tearfully when he finishes. Out of curiosity, I ask why she chose that particular song. She says it was just a random selection based on the fact that it's a song everyone knows.

"Usually I choose the happy birthday song, so I really don't know why I decided on that one."

I explain that baseball is his passion, so it couldn't have been a more perfect choice.

Of course.

Later, Michael's younger sister comes for a visit. I tell her about his etched-in-stone memory of that song. An equally huge Dodgers fan, she relays the sad news about some really good player being traded. His face turns ashen, and out of his mouth pops a very clear, tragically sad "Wow!"

Yep, some memories are for life. Michael, the fan, is certainly still in there.

Getting to 500

After his daily hour of PT today (he walked the halls 15 times with assistance), he gets a second wind and wants to do more.

Excitedly, I take him to the free-time exercise room where he's helped into the standing frame again. Standing in this waist-high wooden box, he starts swaying to his own music.

Shamelessly.

Hamming it up, he veers into an Elvis imitation (usually reserved only for me). The therapists laugh hysterically at this crazy goofball I'm married to.

She then puts him on an adaptive stationary bike that straps in his weak arm and leg so they get exercised simultaneously.

If there's anything in life this man loves it's a challenge. Once he achieves 250 steps he wants to stop, but the therapist says *no, you can get to 500.*

Obediently, he pushes himself hard to get there. Just to prove he can. Or to impress his audience.

Like a teacher acknowledging the best student, PT writes his name and accomplishment on a big chalkboard for all to see. Confidently, she assures that he will reach 1000 steps in a few days.

Big eye roll from Michael, but I know he's taking the challenge seriously. Competition and goals run his life. Apparently, that synapse is still intact.

Love is Real

Today is our 29th wedding anniversary.

Unceremoniously, we sit in our hospital room, holding hands, waiting for his upcoming round of therapy sessions.

Yesterday I took his speech therapist aside and mentioned that this date was special for us. She asked what *Our Song* was, without telling me why.

When she arrives for his session, she notifies Michael that she's downloaded something special on her i-pod.

"You're going to sing this to your wife for your anniversary," she explains.

Not knowing if this particular tune is etched on his inner play list, she clicks on the John Lennon song: *Love is Real.*

As soon as Michael realizes what the song is, he begins singing along. Although the words are Marlon Brando marble mouth, even if John arrived to croon them directly to me, I wouldn't have loved it more.

Tears, of course. I cry and cry. And cry.

Speech therapist cries as well.

There is nowhere else on earth I'd rather be than watching with fascination as my husband is reborn, appreciating every moment of our time together, knowing him better than ever before.

Things that used to annoy me I can't even recall. All the reasons I married this man come flooding back. Clearly, it was the most perfect choice I've ever made in this life. Or any life.

Honestly, this is the best anniversary celebration we've ever shared.

It's such an honor and privilege to take this journey back with the man I love.

Gulp the Glop

After several days eating strictly pureed food, Michael is tested   on swallowing something a bit more solid. He does really well,   so by Monday the glop will be history.

But for now, it's still food as colors.

The highlight of his meal today was a pureed chocolate muffin   for breakfast.

YICH. Could anything be more disgusting?

Yes: The gelatin-thickened water he has to drink.

OMG I'd rather die of thirst.

Different Strokes for Different Folks

Michael is personally invited to attend the "Stroke Inpatient Saturday Wellness Program" today. So, along with eleven other patients, we wheel down to the PT gym to see what they have up their sleeves.

It's fascinating to see the various stages other stroke patients are in. I could choose to feel frustrated at how much further he has to go, but rather, it's providing hope that he will be reaching these stages soon.

After intros and some wheelchair warm up stretches, they hand out a list of twelve events to participate in, giving two hours to accomplish these fetes.

Things like: Make three baskets in a (shortened) basketball hoop; hit a golf ball into a hole; play ping pong; knock bowling pins down; play air hockey and virtual bowl on a Wii video.

Seems like quite a lot of things to do even for someone *not* in a wheelchair.

Given what a sports enthusiast Michael is, I know he'll love doing these activities. It's difficult to tear him away from each station as he tosses, flings and clicks his way through the indoor adaptive games.

Some are frustrating due to his limitations; some are a piece of cake. At every station there's cheering and fist bumps as these small-but-huge challenges are mastered.
Or at least attempted.

At the last event, his personal physical therapist grabs him and offers to do more walking with him. I really think Michael is their pet project, or maybe they just enjoy his ever-present goofiness.

With an enthusiastic YES, he begins going up and down the halls like a pro with lots of assistance. That is, until he has to use the bathroom.

Hurriedly, he's wheeled to the nearest restroom. Thankfully, he actually makes it to the toilet! His own cheering section roars as yet another basket is made, *kerplunk*, with his biggest fan being the loudest! Kobe would be proud.

Afterwards, the rehab group gathers together to share what their favorite activity was. Michael is the only non-verbal participant, so when it's his turn, he indicates through gestures that basketball was his fave.

I'm his personal translator for those not able to understand gesturing.

However, I don't mention his more recent successful basket since it's impolite to boast....

Things to Get Used to in Hospitals

- Endless tests and rarely do they tell you the results (unless they're bad)

- What you think is an emergency is just an everyday occurrence to staff. No, they won't come running when just pee is involved. They move a bit faster if it's poop.

- Being awakened several times in the middle of a dead sleep night, each time the nurse saying: *Mr. Morales, how are you doing?*

Taking a shower using a hospital sink works just fine. Besides, no one cares how stinky you are or that you're wearing the same clothes every single day.

Visitation Rights

So many people want to come and visit Michael, even some we barely know.

Am I being selfish or overly protective telling them not yet? I don't want him to feel on display or for people to feel awkward when the five minutes of trying to get him to talk proves fruitless.

Honestly, I relish our alone time, strictly focusing on his therapy and making sure he doesn't pee on himself.

I guess that's selfish.

Just What the Doctor Ordered

When a speech therapist whom I've never met approaches and asks if Michael is aphasic, I, with my new-found medical word knowledge, give a decided yes.

She probably figures that out when he doesn't answer her himself.

"Does he have any kids?" she asks.

"Well, yes, one, but he's grown. We have grandkids," I explain.

"How old?" she asks.

"Twins, almost eight, and he's their favorite person in the entire world," I answer.

"Have they visited him yet?"

"Nope." I explain that we don't want to freak them out, will wait until he can speak before having them see him.

She looks at me with compassion mixed with pity and says gently, "Well, it might take quite a while for him to be verbal again, and it would be a great idea to have them come visit. They might actually help him speak, maybe read some of their books to him and even play simple games together. He would certainly get inspired seeing them I bet."

Okay, no arm twisting needed to convince me.
Convincing their parents, well, that might be a different story.

Immediately, I text our son who's planning on visiting the next day, relaying what the therapist advised.

Carefully choosing my words, I ask him to "think about" bringing the girls "whenever possible." No mother nudginess or guilt laying from me!

A few minutes later he replies, non-committal about whether he will bring them or not. Heavy sigh. I decide to just trust and see what happens the following day.

The recent death of both their great-grandparents (one actually died from a stroke) has exposed the twins to the impermanency of life early on. One more reason I don't want them to see Michael until we can say, with certainty, he's going to be alright.

This morning at 9:00 a.m. my text beeps: It's my son saying he's bringing the girls. This morning!

I'm so excited I can hardly contain myself. Okay, I don't contain myself. I throw my arms around Michael and tell him the girls are coming to visit!

He seems to kind of understand what I'm talking about, so I hope seeing them will trigger more brain connections. It's so interesting the things his brain is choosing to remember. And not.

An hour later, a showered, clean-shirted, up-in-a-wheelchair, as normal looking as possible G-Pa is ready for his special visitors.

Not sure how prepped they are about what to expect, so I meet them outside for a little debriefing. They seem excited but a little nervous.

I explain that Michael can't speak very well but they can try to help him re-learn his words.

I think of something else. "You know how he always does 'G-Pa gibberish' with you?"

Ever since they were four years old, Michael's been using an incomprehensible language with them that, to everyone else, sounds like a mishmash of Swahili, Yiddish and Martian.

But to the three of them, with various inflections and gestures, the exchange makes perfect sense. They often break into it unexpectedly and can chat that way for extended periods of time. It's adorable. It's their special bond.

"Well, when he talks now it kinda sounds like that," I explain. It seems to ease their concerns.

When they see him waiting in his wheelchair, they eagerly run to hug him. Instantly, a part of him comes back to life. I'm overcome with emotion. Once again.

Excitedly, they take turns wheeling him up and down the hall. All of us go into our room and huddle close around him.

First one, then the other, proudly reads aloud from a collection of Dr. Seuss stories.

Like a child hearing a book for the first time, he's captivated. It seems as if the simple words and drawings make it easy for him to comprehend, even though he understands much more complex things being said. (Note to self: Ask his speech therapist about this.)

The girls take turns drawing pictures on the white board next to his bed, complete with a special loving message for him. Each drawing is of him standing next to them, and they make sure to put his name on it so he knows who it is.

I tell them the other day he sang Take Me Out to the Ballgame, so they sang him the alphabet song and Twinkle Twinkle Little Star (ever notice they are the same tune different words?).
Bobbing his head, he won't sing along. Like most kids, he doesn't like to be put on display or do things on command!

Although they may not understand the depth of what's going on, the girls certainly know how important Michael is in their life.

Their "Geeps" is his silly, child-like self, minus the ability to talk. He becomes their big toy. Not much has changed in that regard.

What a perfect, hands-on way for our girls to learn about compassion, true caring and life challenges.

And to be the best reminder of how much their G-Pa is loved.

Angels with Attitude

At the end of Michael's third day at the acute care hospital ICU, a strapping, sixty-something man walked into our room and identified himself as a "stroke volunteer." He said he was here to talk with us and answer any questions.

I asked the obvious question as to whether he'd had a stroke. "Yes, about five years ago."

Having heard enough of the medical side, I hungered to hear personal experience. "How bad was it?" "How are you now?" "How long did it take you?" "Could you talk?" "Did you know what was going on?"

The more he talked, the more candid he became, making me laugh until I cried as he relayed dead-pan, Cosby-esque stories. Probably only funny to those stroking the same boat.

I learned more from that thirty minute exchange than from any of the medical professionals, and, gratefully, I told him so.

This morning I'm in the rehab hospital dining room to make some tea. There's a twenty-something man struggling, using his good hand to open a Creamora package for his coffee.

I'd noticed him around the halls and in the exercise room, often helping people, just being useful in some capacity. Every time I see him, he seems to glow with true caring.

We say good morning. He moves his coffee and apologizes for being in my way. I tell him he's not in my way since I'm just heating up some water.

He asks how Michael is doing since, apparently, he's noticed us as well.

Without urging, he proceeds to tell me that the reason he's where he is today is because his mother stuck by his side the entire time he was in rehab.

"She was an angel," he explains, "and there were so many times I just wanted to quit and give up but she kept cheering me on."

As he talks I notice his badge. It says "Stroke Volunteer."

We chat for a few more minutes as my water heats up. I ask when he had his stroke. (A year ago). How bad was it. (Really bad). Was he able to talk. (No not at all).

His face gets serious. "Don't give up on your husband; keep on being there for him, no matter what he goes through. He might get frustrated and depressed – that's part of what happens after a stroke – but don't give up!"

He spends several more minutes thanking me for being here. Tearfully of course, I thank him for saying what he said and being an inspiration. Especially since, admittedly, there are fleeting moments when I think *what the heck have I signed up for*.

On the way to physical therapy we bump into this young man again. We wave and share a moment of connected eye contact.

The physical therapist pushing Michael's wheelchair shoots a couple of wise cracks his direction, and they fist-bump happily.

Once he's out of earshot, PT tells us that this man was probably the most difficult patient he's ever dealt with.

"He was stubborn, mean, and would threaten to walk out and not do his exercises," he explains. "I had to chase him down a couple of times because he actually bolted!"

Yikes.

"Wow. And look at him now," I say, amazed at his physical healing and, even more at how sweet, kind, and caring he's become.

I speculate that a stroke was this man's personal transformative experience.

The Universe, in its infinite wisdom, sure knows how to rock people's boats so they can get whatever they're supposed to get, eh?

So, what am I supposed to be getting from all this?

Well, the list is long and grows longer daily. But the short list is: Even deeper levels of trust, compassion, caring. Patience. Communicating without words.

And then there's good ol' commitment. A vow I made to Michael 29 years ago and plan on keeping. *In sickness and...*

Like I said, just a few.

Sure glad I've been working on these for dozens of years so I'm ready to delve deeper, making them even more real and ever-present.

What's the Secret?

This morning, Michael's favorite nurse Eric cleans him up and helps him get ready for his busy, non-stop therapy day.

This guy is big, probably late thirties, very on top of things, and also quite the character. Witty. Droll. Same sense of humor Michael has, even without the ability to speak.

Daily, they banter back and forth, Michael giving looks that say it all.

Probably even better than with words.

Making small talk with me, Eric asks how long we've been married. "Twenty nine years as of this past Saturday."

"What's The Secret?" he asks, genuinely wanting to know. Apparently, he's in the middle of a contentious divorce.

Without missing a beat, I reply: *"Communication."*

Five seconds of silence until we realize the irony of my answer. We burst into hysterical laughter!

Maybe because of our long history, or maybe because we have an amazing psychic connection (you wouldn't have wanted to play Charades against us!), even without speech, we're able to completely understand each other. Most of the time.

Now, when Michael wants something, it usually only takes a slight Neanderthal grunt for me to figure out what he's asking for.

If he's upset about something, I can feel it without him uttering a sound. If he's annoyed at a situation, well, let's just say it doesn't take more than a slight eye roll for me to read his thoughts.

And, the same is true on his end.

I've never hidden anything from him, no matter how difficult to admit, ugly, uncomfortable or embarrassing.

Even now, when it's vitally important I remain positive, holding back is not an option. I know he doesn't want me to, and even if he did, it's virtually impossible for me to even attempt to be fake.

If I'm in the middle of fear, anger, or frustration and not able to be his Susie Sunshine cheerleader, the only way to return to my 'good place' is to talk about what's going on.

Luckily, it doesn't take much, just a quick verbal acknowledgment of where I'm at, and immediately I'm fine.

Really fine.

So, I guess even without the privilege of speech, communication is The Secret.

Uno, Dos, Tres

One of the things they offer rehab patients at Rancho is something called "Recreation Therapy." Who knew there's a college major where you can actually get a job doing fun things with people all day! Next life, that's my gig.

Unless I stick to my original plan to be a rock star. (Gotta plan ahead, right?)

Today we have our first RT session. His therapist, Anna, twenty five if she's a day and quite serious about her work, asks Michael what he wants to do.

Since he doesn't speak, she gives him three choices: Art, games or sports. Without a moment's hesitation, wild head nod selects games.

Michael is highly competitive. Life and death cutthroat, to be exact. Add that to a gotta-follow- the- rules- to- a- tee, it used to be hard to find people willing to play games with him. In fact, the last time we had game night at our house, several friends walked out in a huff, never wanting to come back.

He's almost "taken his baseball bat and gone home" as well, even when I remind him, *it's just a game and we are supposed to be having fun.* He can't seem to get past his terminator attitude.

So, when shown a closet shelf full of games and he selects UNO as his recreational therapy of choice, I relax. *Honestly, how competitive can he possibly get playing this simple, early child-level game?*

The therapist deals seven cards to each of us, giving him a wooden slotted card holder contraption since he has no use of his right hand.

At first he's confused, can't figure out what to do, doesn't even know which numbers match. But within minutes, he catches on, and also within minutes, beats both of us! Not once, but twice!

We play a total of six games, his therapist and I only winning two. Witnessing his combative fangs coming out, I'm glad the hour is up.

Anna offers to let us borrow the deck so we can play in our room. The minute we get back, that's all he wants to do.

As we play, his moves became more strategic. Planning ahead. Figuring out ways to beat me. Seriously competing.

It's interesting to note that the competitive spirit lives on even after a stroke. Must be hardwired in that brain somewhere.

If there's a gene I'm missing, it's the competitive one. But, I find myself trying harder and harder to beat him. Not so I can win, but to push him a bit, fire up the old noodle and snap those synapsis into attention again.

He beams. Even though I beat him twice, he knows he accomplished something. Big.

Each game we play puts wider grins on my face. I'm chuckling. Then laughing. Joyously.

Pondering why, I realize that this reminds me of times I used to play UNO with my son when he was really little. We would play for hours, even though it's probably the most boring game (besides Candyland) ever invented. It's one of those sweet memories you don't realize you're making until 38 (gulp) years later.

Sadly, I also realize I haven't sat still and relaxed long enough to play non-thinking games like this in just as many decades.

The only games Michael and I used to play were word games on our cell phones. We played them during stolen moments between customers, or lying in bed before drifting off to sleep. When we occasionally had friends over for game nights, it was certainly not relaxing!

Sitting here with nothing else to do except focus completely on this silly game feels like floating and bobbing on a cruise ship, stretched out on a deck chair, drink in one hand. Relaxing. Being completely present, in the moment. Taking it all in because, after all, you're on VACATION.

This might be a different kind of vacation, but being with my husband as his brain wakes up couldn't be a more enjoyable and interesting trip.

And waking up it is. Maybe by the time we dock?

Competition Stays Forever

After his success playing Uno, we join in with a group of stroke patients playing Mexican Bingo ("Loteria"), another recreational therapy event.

Within minutes, Michael is peaking at everyone's cards to make sure he isn't losing. Luckily there's no skill involved or it could've been an insurrection.

Every time he gets a match for one of the pictures in his hand, he makes a fist and grunts "Yeaha!" like he has money riding on the game.

The others in the group are enjoying playing, but it's becoming life and death to win for Michael.

After three rounds, losing each time, Michael retrieves a new word for his ever-expanding vocabulary: *Damn.*

Should I wash his mouth out with soap or be thrilled he lassoed yet one more word?

It's So Easy to Fall in Love

This morning, Michael's physical therapist tells us that we'll be focusing on learning to do things we'll be doing at home. So we can feel more confident.

(Home? We're going home?)

PT spends the entire hour teaching me how to help Michael get from his wheelchair to the toilet and back again.

All I can say is: They sure make it look easy.

It takes about six times to finally get in the flow, so to speak, but I still feel ten thumbs clumsy.

It's all about making sure the wheelchair is positioned right, having his butt forward on the chair, bending my knees, bracing him on his weak leg with my knees, grabbing the back of his pants, having his hand holding the locked wheelchair or the railing, making sure his weak foot is positioned correctly, having him stand straight and not attempting to do any of this until I say *"Ready: One, two, three."*

Oh, and doing any self-corrections once he's standing or trying to sit so he doesn't fall and take me with him!

Easy pee-sie, right?

As I struggle with the lesson, secretly feeling less confident with each transfer, PT assures me that he too felt that way for a long time. In fact, he confides, he's dropped patients many

times. No big deal. *It's all part of the process; it's all just a learning experience.* For them and for him.
Easy for him to say.

The rest of our day is learning through having fun. We go to a cooking class (vegetarian of course) where Michael gets to chop up vegies using a one-hand converted cutting board that grips what he's trying to cut.

He then peels carrots using another adaptive device. I can see the wheels turning in that logical mind of his, redesigning the contraptions so they're even better to use.

Or finding an easier way.

He ends up doing everything the teacher instructs but in his own way. He listens politely, spends a minute pondering the task, and comes up with a different way to do it.

The Michael Way. Just like he used to do everything.

His face beams with delight proving the teacher wrong. Hiding her frustration, she gives up and says, *hey, do whatever works for you!*

That's how he's always been. Good quality to have and even better now.

At the end of the day, we mosey back to our room and he indicates he has to use the toilet. "Number one or number two?" I ask.

He points to his butt and I get the Number two message loud and clear. This is still a pretty exciting triumph since only a few days ago he wasn't aware of that bodily function.

Given past experience, when he tells me he has to go, he REALLY has to go. Badly.

To save time, I wheel him into the bathroom and push the nurse call button for help. I'm still not certified to do transfers alone.

Word of advice: Never need a nurse STAT when they are changing shifts. Bad timing.

We wait and wait and wait some more. I stroke his head and say hold on, be patient, you can wait, and anything else I can think of to assure that he'll be fine.

Meanwhile, I practice my morning transfer training by positioning his wheelchair correctly, putting his feet in the proper pose, untying his hospital pants and taking off the seatbelt. Anything to save time for the nurse.

This ten minute eternity finally ends when Eric, his favorite nurse, comes to the rescue. He takes one look at how I have the wheelchair positioned, explains it's actually supposed to face the other way, and quickly yanks it to the correct angle.

Before I'm able warn him that Michael's seatbelt is unfastened, like a sack of potatoes, off he tumbles, plunging to the floor. We both jump to prevent the fall to no avail.

Splat.

Eric is a big guy. He easily scoops him up and plunks him on the toilet seat without a second thought.

Michael's head is in his hands and I can't tell if he's laughing or crying, injured or not.

"Are you okay? Are you okay? Are you hurt?" I ask frantically. When he finally looks up, his face is shocked but he's smiling that goofy Michael grin.
As relieved as I'm shaken, tears burst through my Wonder Woman façade. The nurse turns his attention to the sniveling wife and assures me Michael is fine.

Crying now out of control. I know better than try to suppress it.

Walking quickly out of the bathroom, crying inching close to hysteria.

Super Nurse follows behind, grabs me lovingly by the shoulders and says emphatically, "No crying, he's fine, this happens. A lot."

Choking out, *yes, I know, but he's been through so much I just don't want him to go through anything else. Especially more physical pain.*

Looking directly in my eyes, hugging me hard, Eric offers infinite wisdom: "You know, it's all just a learning experience."

Didn't I just hear that this morning?

When words stick like that and a few hours later get shoved in my face again, I figure the Universe is giving me a message.

A pretty obvious one: *Get stronger, everything is a learning experience,* and, *on the count of one two three: You're ready.*

What You Don't Know Won't Hurt You

Whenever I would go out for a meal with my Mother, she'd shake her head, make a tsk tsk sound and roll her eyes when I'd ask the server if the soup was made with vegetarian stock.

She would say, quote, *If you don't know whether it's vegetarian, it's okay to eat it!*

I would roll my eyes back at her *don't-ask, don't-care* philosophy. Eventually, I gave up trying to explain why this committed vegetarian wanted to know what's in her food.

Today the Recreation Therapist asks Michael what he wants to do in their session together. He's not sure, so once again she takes us into her storeroom, letting him rummage through games, sporting supplies and other in sundry items.

The minute he sees a shelf with jigsaw puzzles, his face lights up. This is clearly his treatment du jour.

Michael has Buddha-esque patience, able to sit for hours putting together 2000 piece jigsaw puzzles. Days, if he had the time. Luckily he never did. Nor would I let him, task master that I am.

Always more important things to do. Like run a shop.

The three of us traipse off to sit at an outdoor table (ah fresh air!), a bit brisk, but it's December in SoCal tolerable.

Minutes later, the 200 piece dinosaur puzzle he chose is spread out face up before him.

It starts out fine. Without prompting, he finds all the straight edge pieces and corners, lines them up and starts matching them.

Now, in the not too distant past, this challenge would've been an insult to his puzzle prowess, an affront to his jigsaw propensity. In fact, he undoubtedly would've finished it in a snap.

But post stroke is different.

The struggle begins. Pain filled face, furrowed brow, head in hands kind of struggle. Therapist and wife get concerned. "Are you okay?" we both ask simultaneously.

He shakes his head no.

"What's going on?" we both ask. "Are you in pain?"

Another no.

A few questions later, we determine that he's just very, very frustrated.

Therapist asks if he wants to stop. If there's one thing Michael is not it's a quitter. His head automatically shakes no. He rests a minute and forges on.

Pain filled, furrowed brow, head in hands again.

"Michael you're doing a great job," praises Anna.

It doesn't matter what she says. It's obvious that, in his mind, because he's not able to do it effortlessly like before, he

believes he's failing. And, that is absolutely unacceptable in Michael's self-determined world.
So he pushes forward and continues.

After almost an hour, he accomplishes finishing the entire border, all three corners (the fourth was missing from the box) and almost half the sky. To us it's quite a fete; to him another reminder of what he's now incapable of doing effortlessly.

To end on a more positive note, the therapist says "Let's play UNO!" knowing how much he loved it the other day. Unfortunately, it's a fast game with Anna beating us both.

So much for that idea.

We go back inside to his speech therapy session. He usually brightens up the minute he hears the unmistakable sound of her keys jingling down the hall. However, today, nothing she says or does pulls him from the funk of puzzle failure.

I tell her what happened and she explains that, in a weird way, that's a good sign.

"He's starting to be aware of what he DOESN'T know and CAN'T do, and it's bothering him. It's not like a child who's excitedly learning everything brand new. He already knows all this but can't access it and it's starting to be frustrating." *Kind of like ignorance is bliss, right?*

"Yep," she says.

I more than get it.

Confession time. I'm one of those people who arrived on this earth with lots of awareness. So much so that I was overly sensitive, empathetic to what others were feeling.

You name it. Sadness, loneliness, pain, fear, and even more so, the condition of the world: War, poverty, hunger, intolerance, injustice, racism.

As a '60's teenager, I became an "activist," protesting everything one could protest. And there was a lot.

It was frustrating and empowering, simultaneously.

But every night in the privacy of my psychedelic, flower-power, peace-symbol filled orange and lime green bedroom, I would curl up in fetal position and pray to not be conscious. The pain was monumental and I didn't know what to do with it.

Begging, I would plead, to whoever the gods in charge of such things were, to be unaffected by what I was observing around me.

I longed for ignorance so I could *ignore* it all.

Thank goodness the answer to those prayers was a resounding demonstrative *NO, sorry, not this time.* Why? Because from that empathic pain came deep compassion and ultimately the insatiable need to help others.

And myself.

Eventually, that's what birthed my spiritually-based, self-development teachings in 1977.

But now, watching Michael re-awaken from his ignore-ance, it's reminding me of times wanting to stick fingers in ears, close eyes tightly and say *Lalalalala!*

There's nothing I can do to prevent it, nor do I want to. But witnessing him go from a blissfully content Happy Place, to a Not So Happy *Aware* Place is like watching a giggling baby go warp speed to fully cognizant adult.

Without a seat belt.

Maybe my Mother was right: *If you don't know what's in that soup you're ordering, it does make it okay to eat it.*

Nah.

Level Playing Field

One of the first "skills" Michael regained was in post-acute care at the hospital. I left his room for a few minutes to grab something to eat in the downstairs cafeteria. By the time I got back, he'd re-figured out how to use the TV remote.

Picture this: He's utterly helpless, no right side movement, non-verbal, unable to swallow or use the toilet, but somehow still master of his precious remote. He actually somehow located a football game and was gleefully watching every play!

If he could've, I'm sure he would've been cheering each touchdown, explaining once again the rules of this game I hate. Yawn.

I guess some skills exist in the brain's motherboard. Without sounding sexist, should I say male brains?

Can you tell I'm at the other end of the spectrum when it comes to sports? In fact, it's one of our (few) ongoing marriage 'issues:' Michael wants to watch a game, any game (they're all the same to me!), and I don't.

We have one TV and one remote. Hmmm... guess who wins?

Thank the tech gods for inventing TIVO!

Saturday mornings at Rancho, no therapy and absolutely nothing to do. I'm tortured by game after game that Michael insists on watching. When he dozes off, I sneak to his bed and try to snatch the remote from his death grip. He wakes up.

"Noooo!" and grabs it back.

Without the benefits of mind-numbing television, I read and work on my writing. It's almost impossible for me to concentrate with the sounds of cheering cranked full volume.

Finally, it's time to attend the weekly Inpatient Wellness Program. This week's theme is "Spirit" (as in mind, body and...). Just my cuppa tea being a spiritual teacher and all.

The Recreation Therapist starts out by showing a film of adaptive (seated) Tai Chi. The narrator has us all slowly, rhythmically moving our bodies to his simple commands.

Neither of us has ever done this type of exercise, and it's delightful to combine stretching with moving energy (chi) around.

Twelve patients and a few visitors sit in a circle, synchronously doing these movements, mostly in wheelchairs, some with walkers.

The group is diverse: Patients from thirty to close to eighty, male, female, every culture and demographic, all intensely engrossed in trying to do even the easiest of stretches. If they have movement in both limbs, it makes it easier, but even those who don't, figure out creative ways to adapt.

These all walks of life people fill the room with one commonality: Stroke.

When the DVD is finished, the therapist changes the mood by passing out musical instruments to everyone.

Rain sticks, drums, bells, tom-toms, castanets, and weird plastic things that make a clicking sound when you wave them.

Like a group of preschoolers, we hold our instruments in eager anticipation, waiting to find out what to do with them. "Okay," she explains, "everyone's going to say how they feel and then express it with their instrument!"

It's remarkable that most everyone in the circle names the same feeling: Happy. Michael parrots everyone's response and shakes his tambourine to emphasize.

As I look at their glowing, being-in-the-present-moment faces, they truly are happy.

Even though post-stroke.

She then asks for song suggestions and boy does she get 'em! Ranging from Christmas music to rap and everything in between, we play our instruments to whatever beat blasts at us.

The other therapists in attendance spontaneously jump up and dance, pulling up some of the more mobile patients and gently sway with them.

It's just as therapeutic as the "official" work they do, disguised as fun.

Each person is completely absorbed in making their own music. Using a plastic drumstick, Michael hits his tambourine attentively, like it's the most important thing he could ever be doing.

Having use of both arms, I'm given cymbals and get to make some serious, shameless noise!

I look around at this group of brave, strong people each going through this unanticipated Big Life Challenge.

There's no distinction between where they're from, their education level, economic status or background. Each is a temporary resident in the same rehab boat, each wearing the same frumpy, tied-in-the-back gown, flattened bed-hair, several days of beard, and not a drop of makeup to hide behind.

Each with one common denominator: Healing.

Kind of like our temporary residency in life (but with a bit more grooming, hopefully).

Of course, it moves me to unabashed tears, letting them pour onto my jeans, not wanting to miss a beat with my cymbals.

Staff is getting used to my daily waterworks displays and they don't miss a beat either.

Physical challenges certainly bring out the best in people. And, without a doubt, puts us all on a level playing field.

Which, really, we already are.

Wouldn't it be nice to see life this way out of the rehab boat?

For me it starts by letting Michael watch some ball being kicked around on some level playing field in our room for the rest of the day... without complaint. He earned it by playing that tambourine so skillfully.

Come Out, Come Out, Wherever You Are!

One of the most fascinating things about the kind of stroke Michael had is that thought processes, intelligence, knowledge, skills, memories and desires are in there, but they just can't be expressed.

At least not in a discernable way.

It's like a turtle locked inside a shell, poking its head out occasionally, but not long enough to have a full conversation or to even tell them anything important.

In the last few days, random words have popped out, surprising us both. He knows when he says them correctly, and it's thrilling!

Today he said: *Thank you; I know; Yeah; Wow; (a very emphatic) Don't help me; I don't want that; and What's the problem!*

His speech therapist gave him homework to count to five at least ten times a day, and he proudly counted to ten! All things that show he's undeniably emerging from the shell he's trapped in.

Slowly but surely, tortoise is beating hare.

Which leads me to the story of Pokey, a six inch desert tortoise my grandfather gave me when I was about eight years old.

Although (understatement) Pokey didn't do much – couldn't teach him tricks or train him in any way –

I loved that unhurried, wise looking, very quiet reptile. Maybe it gave me 'cool points' to have a pet none of my friends had. Maybe it was the challenge of trying to connect with something that clearly didn't care anything at all about me.

Or anyone else for that matter, as far as I could tell.

My mother had no idea where to put him, so he was assigned the "run" of the backyard. Soon after, he adopted a small geranium bush as his hiding place. I would go outside and watch him, giving him lettuce and an occasional apple treat.

Wasn't quite sure what to feed him, but he didn't seem to care about that either. The yard was a gated area that was completely tortoise proof.

So I thought.

One day after school, it was time for some tortoise face time. Searching his usual haunts, I couldn't find hair nor shell of him.

After twenty minutes and no Pokey to be found, I panicked.

Running inside I screamed, "Mommy, POKEY IS MISSING!"

My mother, who cared as much about this reptile as he did about her, disinterestedly looked up from her newspaper, confident that I would find him.

"Well, he couldn't have gone too far," she assured, tongue firmly planted in cheek. She didn't offer to help; I was on my own.

I went outside and searched again, checking under the geranium bush to see if he had tunneled his way out somehow.   Or his brown/green shell had somehow been camouflaged.

Despondently, I gave up and went inside to do my homework.
At dinner my mother stated her theory. "I think Pokey ran away," she explained.

The preposterousness of that couldn't get past even an eight year old. "Ran away?" I said. "How could he do that? He's so slow, and how could he have gotten out of the gate?"

She shrugged off my questions with one of those *knowing mother* smiles. At that age I still believed that mothers knew everything, so without further questioning, I accepted her explanation.

Possibly she was glad to not have to feed a creature that would probably outlive her.

I cried myself to sleep that night, missing my hard-shelled friend, envisioning his sluggish, crinkly legs racing up the street, dodging cars, avoiding capture.

The next morning I posted signs all over the neighborhood: "LOST: POKEY, A SIX INCH BROWN AND GREEN TORTOISE! If found, please call VE8-7725." No one did.

In the first year of our marriage, I relayed that story to Michael, still brushing a tear from my cheek at the tragic end.

Michael looked at me in astonishment, not even attempting to suppress a grin.

Instead of giving sympathy for my childhood trauma, he said with conviction: "Royce, there is no way Pokey ran away. I bet your mom actually ran him over and just didn't want to tell you!"

Gasping, I nearly fell over.

No. He's wrong. Would my mother do something like that? Could I have been that naïve? Images of a Pokey Pancake danced through my head.

"No. No way. She wouldn't have done that!"
Admittedly, my defense was half-hearted: Michael's explanation actually made more sense than my mother's.

Thoughts of Pokey plotting to escape his backyard prison, scurrying off to make his way in the world, flooded my mind.

Although not at all funny, I laughed at how absurd it was. It became one of our private jokes. Michael needed only to glance over at me when I was about to gullibly believe something ridiculous and say one word under his breath: Pokey.

He was always right.

So now, when I see my wisely perceptive husband stuck in his own tortoise shell prison, I think about all he's going to say when he emerges completely.
Especially when he reads all I've posted on Facebook and wants to tuck his head safely back in!

Or run up the street to escape....

I still can't believe my mother ran over Pokey. *No. Way.*

Downtime?

I used to think I was the most patient person on the planet, until I met Michael. Compared to his beyond sainthood persevering ability, my lack of fortitude was shameful.

In ways only someone close to you (and with permission to be brutally honest) can do, he'd lovingly point out my impatience. Frequently.

I always had my reasons (what he called justifications), but trying to argue was pointless since, as stated previously, Michael is always right.

Yes, I admit it, he is.

Today, Sunday, when there's still nothing to do at the rehab hospital, I start going a little stir crazy.

With no therapy sessions, nowhere to eat, and no visitors, I try to fill up our time with something, anything, that will be somewhat therapeutic.

Why? Undoubtedly selfish motives: I'm impatiently wanting my husband back.

Michael, on the other hand, is happy just chillin,' still watching endless football games.

"Let's take a walk," I suggest. Michael barely looks up from the tube and shrugs his shoulders. "Nah," he says. He's mastered a few words with 'nah' being one of his most perfected.

Thirty minutes later I suggest it again. A bit more insistently. And again. And yet again.

Finally he relents.

Excitedly, I run to the nursing station to get some help. Together, we put his tennis shoes on, change into a clean shirt, comb his hair and have him use the toilet.

This takes about an hour, give or take.

Loading him onto his wheelchair, off we go.

Just about skipping down the hall, we pass the front desk and let the attendant know we're going for a walk. "We'll be back," I promise, gleefully. She knows we will.

Emerging outside into the 75 degree, December afternoon, we breathe in the non-recycled hospital air. Wheeling over to a courtyard filled with bare winter trees, we sit at a rusty metal picnic table with a seat conveniently removed for wheelchair access. They sure think of everything here!

Although we haven't left each other's side for almost a month, there hasn't been much talk about anything "important."

Like our store. Or our future.

Casually, I decide to broach both subjects. He tries hard to focus on what I'm saying, but clearly he isn't able to.

Maybe not the best subject choices for a first tête-à-tête.

Within minutes, he's clearly overwhelmed. Evidently, I'm still needing to learn what he can and can't listen to.

After ten minutes outside, he indicates he's ready to return to the room. Sauntering, I take the long way back, hoping he won't notice.

Since his stroke, Michael notices the most inconsequential details. Even slight changes in routine or his environment are bothersome. So, until we finally get back to the safety of his room, he's anxious.

Surrendering, I decide to simply allow him his day of rest. After all, most people are allowed a day or two off a week, just not retail shop owners. Still in that mode.

Impatience is once again getting the better of me.

Post Day of Rest

Monday's schedule more than makes up for Sunday's down time. Michael has five total hours of therapy, starting promptly at 9:00 a.m., with a one hour break for lunch.

Miraculously, it's his most productive day thus far!

He's starting to have hip movement which allows for some movement in his right leg. He leads the way as we both master transferring from his wheelchair to various locations (such as a practice car). He stands for several minutes in the standing box, and obeys the therapist when told to march (extemporaneously singing his own marching song as only wacky Michael can!).

But the most exciting part happens in speech therapy.

Since his stroke almost a month ago, Michael has only said a few random words at arbitrary times. Like a child being put on display, he rarely talks when asked to, only when he feels like it. Words pop out on their own volition and he's as surprised as I am when they do.

However, today, with a different therapist, I witness the list expand exponentially.

She discovers that if she shows him a picture of something and then writes the word under it, he's able to say what it is!

This is remarkable and, of course, moves me to tears. (Never a dry-eyed day!) The therapist is equally shocked and thrilled since it's so unexpected.

Clearly, he's trying super hard and responds well to her no nonsense approach. Mirroring how he was with himself pre-stroke, this therapist shows little patience with mistakes or with him giving up.

Or his impatience with himself.

Hmmm. Maybe Michael just needed an impatient little kick in the butt, or maybe a day of rest.

Or maybe both.

Wack-a-Doodle

It dawns on me that Michael isn't laughing. It's weird since so much of his pre-stroke time was spent either laughing at something or making others laugh. Even in the acute care hospital, unable to do much of anything, he easily made others laugh just by facial expressions and gestures.

It's one of those in-the-face-reality moments, made worse realizing I don't remember what his laugh sounds like.

Yikes.

Before Michael entered my life, I believed that one of my best qualities was how serious, studious, and intellectual I was. My Mother was a certified genius, so I was raised thinking those qualities were of paramount importance.

It used to be fun getting into intellectual debates with people, feeling good at how many facts I could espouse, gratified to out-logic anyone on most any topic. (Confession: I could even fake it fairly well on topics I knew nothing much about.)

Once I started exploring spirituality, those qualities took a back seat as I discovered even more important things: Acceptance, love, compassion, caring, connection, truth, trust, openness, and forgiveness.

They become primary goals to achieve, since I wasn't adept at any of them (to put it mildly).

The spiritual road I traversed started out a gentle slope, but as I got more committed, the incline steepened, offering some tough life lessons. It was easy to mouth pretty, Higher

Consciousness concepts, much more difficult to actually live them. It was an obvious difference, and I was only satisfied with authenticity.

After a number of years navigating my inner journey, I discovered another quality that not only equaled those states of being, but surpassed them.

The quality was JOY.

Realizing I had bypassed its importance demonstrated that I was in dire need of some *serious* joy in my life.

I'd been divorced from my first husband for about ten years, looking diligently for my Mr. Right. After a less than ideal marriage, my decree became: *No settling.*

Each man I dated was able to fulfill some qualities on my fairly lengthy Wish List, but no one filled the bill entirely.

Until Michael.

If you were limited to using one word to describe him, it would have to be 'funny.' His humor ranges from clever/droll to slapstick/wacky. And everywhere between.

What I loved most about him was how he could be doing the most ridiculous, child-like thing, and a minute later shift into profound seriousness.

After the first few days of his stroke, his repertoire of silly faces would show up during even the most trying times. Nurses and doctors would break into giggles as this zany guy would mess with them, even without the benefit of speech.

My sense is that, once his wacky is completely out, laughter and all, it will mean he's more completely healed. Today demonstrates that we're getting closer to attaining full-on goofy.

It starts during his daily two minute exam by the resident doctor. She uses a stethoscope and listens to his heart, both in the front of his chest and back.

When she does this she asks him to say AHHH.

Yesterday, he was finally able to follow her command and get the sound out perfectly. However, today, when requesting the same thing, he says ahh, ahh, ahh and then a deliberate, sheepish BAHH!

The doctor and I both crack up, and Michael deadpans a look that says, *what's so funny?*

His next comedic routine arrives when I'm being instructed how to give him a "bed bath." He lays there, naked as a jaybird, unembarrassed as I clean all his parts (okay, never in a million years did I think I'd be cleaning my husband's butt).

Suddenly, he begins hamming it up, singing loud enough for the entire hospital floor to hear. Just like being alone in the shower.

Side-splitting laughter stops this bath mid rinse. I throw in the towel. Literally. On his face.

The entire day he has therapists and nurses in stitches (maybe not a good hospital word choice). But the ultimate hilarity occurs during speech therapy.

Speaking is still his biggest challenge, but he says volumes with his eyes and facial expressions.

Now that words are flowing a little easier, he decides to try out his comedic repartee with his favorite speech therapist, Randy. The two of them already have quite the banter together, but today takes the proverbial cake.

It starts with us making a list of potential things Michael could be trying to ask for. Basic things such as food, toilet, bed, and of course the TV remote.

Next, we make a list of "I ams" – I am tired; I am hungry; I am sleepy; I am sad, etc.

Last, she asks for the names of people close to him, family, friends, or anyone he might want to ask about.

When I mention a particular name (I will never disclose who), he makes a face and clearly says 'ick.' We all laugh, and when the therapist has him try to say all the names on the sheet, the only one he can't/won't say is this particular person.

And, it's one of the easier ones to pronounce.

He's doing it on purpose. To be funny.

We laugh until we cry.

At the end of their session, without prompt, he says the clearest two words he has yet to speak, directly to this therapist: *Merry Christmas!*

All three of us, including Michael, laugh long and hard.
His laugh is back.

The therapist, who's leaving for two weeks on a winter
vacation, says something I will always cherish: "Michael, you
have my heart."

And, from one who feels the same way, welcome back Mr.
Silly Stuff! I've missed that laugh more than anything else in
the world.

For Pity's Sake!

It's Christmas eve, exactly one month since Michael's stroke. Time to get all dolled up in my holiday best and go out to my very own pity party. I hear they are well attended this time of year. Didn't think I would be attending one, but I guess I am.

It starts when I find out that our almost eight year old twin granddaughters aren't able to visit tomorrow. Which means our son won't be coming. And, since they are the hosts of the family Christmas dinner, I guess there won't be any family visiting here at all.

Which, although slightly disappointing, is actually just fine.

It's cozy-comfortable in our little hospital cocoon. With no therapy and nothing to do because of the holiday, we can relax, watch football all day (yippee-icky!) and take in some serious chill time.

But, 'tis the season for sentimentality, so rationalizations don't prevent making reservations at the nearest Poor Me celebration. TG it's an itsy bitsy party that doesn't last too long.

How can it when I know I'm not a victim of circumstance?

I exit the party abruptly when my attention goes to something more pressing than just another 25th day in December: Michael's inability to control urination, knowing when it's urgent and when it's a false alarm. (Insert gruesome visual of your choice here!)

After dinner, when Michael "loses it" (so to speak), I nearly get a whiplash snapping back to what's truly important. So, when I see him RSVP-ing to attend his *own* pity party, I give him The Pep Talk that's word-for-word what I should've given myself earlier.

Actually, it's what he would've been giving me if able to get words out.

After cleaning him up, I stand close by his bedside. Stroking his hair, I remind him that his body is still trying to adjust to getting correct messages from his brain. I remind him how far he's come in a month.

I remind him that this is no big deal.

I remind him about when our granddaughters were learning how to be potty trained: They made some mistakes as their bodies adjusted to the signals. No big deal.

It takes a minute, but I realize we're doing what I refer to as "See-sawing."

Here's how it works: Everything is energy. You can try pushing down the energy of emotions, fears, lies, etc. but, like the non-negotiable law of gravity, it doesn't work.

There's even a Law of Physics stating that "nothing can ever be suppressed."

The more something is pushed down, the more it must come up somewhere else, in some form, often when we least expect it, and more often than not, in those closest to us.

Imagine trying to force a completely filled, tightly knotted balloon to stay at the bottom of a pool. The more you force it, the more it pops up.

The same phenomenon occurs when we suppress things going on inside ourselves. Like hiding our anger; denying our fears; withholding a lie, or, ahem, ignoring feeling sorry for ourselves.

The relationship Michael and I have is based on not giving each other pity, but rather, supporting each other in more empowering ways.

Giving pity is actually quite addictive. It's the socially accepted way we're taught to define love *("If you love me you need to feel really bad for whatever I'm going through rather than lovingly supporting me in understanding what my lessons are.")*.

Pity is as thick as the quicksand-like glop Michael had to eat when he couldn't swallow. As we wildly flail to get out of it, or deny feeling it, it sucks us in deeper.

So today, as I made my grand entrance into the Feeling Sorry For Myself Holiday Gala (which really meant I was just feeling afraid), instead of acknowledging what was going on to Michael, I'd stuffed it.

Here's my inner dialogue: *Oh, Royce, you shouldn't feel this way. After all, it's Christmas and you know they'd visit if they could. What's with all the poor me stuff? Just be happy!*

So, guess what? Minutes later, Michael comes crashing down into his own pity partay.
Understanding the see-saw phenomena helps me not get trapped in negativity for too long. Having the other end of the seesaw fly up and hit me in the face often enough has taught me well.
It can happen in the blink of an eye, or as fast as suppressing and rationalizing my sadness about not seeing my family at Christmas.

Anyway, two miraculous gifts arrive that are even better: Michael very clearly and deliberately says "I love you!"

Plus, because Michael is making such phenomenal progress, working diligently to improve, they extend his rehab stay another ten days! That's how it works.
Couldn't be a better present for both of us!

Random Regrets

Regrets come a flying when you realize that someone you love may not ever be back again in the same form.

Like, why didn't I listen more closely to what he was saying, the stories he told me, his jokes?

Like, why can't I remember all the skills he taught me, the power tools he instructed me to use, the way he hammers nails without smashing his thumb each time?

Like, why did we waste even a minute being angry with each other, whether over something insignificant or important?

Regrets, misgivings, remorse, and whatever else you want to label them really suck. Especially since there's nothing you can do about them.

Except learn.

And not waste any more time.

Promise.

Clichés of Truth

About three a.m. I wake up having an intense "nightmare." I put that word in quotes because it feels far too real to just be a dream.

Even though "nightmare" implies "bad," I know they are just wake up calls (pardon the pun) to give a swift kick in the butt about something being avoided.

I'm sure Freud would have his way with it, but to me, this dream is more of an actual experience, especially since I rarely, if ever, have such intense dreams.

In the dream, someone's putting a pillow over my face, violently trying to suffocate me. I feel the realness of the pillow, the weight of this person pushing it down, and I'm literally not able to breath.

Struggling to find my voice to scream for help, and, when I'm finally able, it comes out in a minuscule squeak. Eventually I'm able to yell loud enough for the nursing station to hear. But, rather than wait for them to save me, I force myself to wake up, check to see if there's a pillow over my face, calm my pounding heart and drift off to sleep again.

Now, if you ascribe to the traditional viewpoint that dreams are just symbolic, with every character being an aspect of self, then the meaning is pretty evident: I feel like I'm suffocating myself and can't get my voice out to ask for help.

Obvious, right?

In my spiritual classes I teach that the dreamer is the only accurate interpreter; there's no 'pat analysis' to be found in dream dictionaries. Also, dreams can be multidimensional, meaning we can be out of our bodies, participating in realms we know nothing about in our awake state. Happens a lot, but we seem to forget those quickly.

Assuming the standard dream analysis is accurate, I have to ponder if part of me does feel that way.

Hmmm.

Even though I believe the adage "We are never given more than we can handle," maybe there's been some sort of cosmic mix up.

Did the Universe get the wrong address this time?

During these weeks of hospitals and rehab, admittedly, a few times I doubted whether I'd be able to handle everything piled on my overflowing my plate.

But, daily I feel more confident, capable of doing whatever it takes to not only take care of Michael, but to continue doing whatever I'm supposed to be doing in life.

Not sure exactly what that will look like, but trusting I'll know when the time comes.

The life I've chosen has honed my skills of trusting, going with the flow and living 'in the mystery.' Clearly, everything I've gone through thus far has been 'prep work" for all I'm going through now.

Even in obscure ways, ways that didn't make sense until Michael's stroke.

Like feeling compelled to join a gym and work out hard these last three years with no clue as to why (now I'm fit enough to help him in and out of his wheelchair).

Or when the Universe surprisingly, for no apparent reason, "forced" me to walk away from some big things that were draining financially (there's no way I would be able to maintain them now).

Daily, more reasons emerge as to the Divine Timing of this experience that's been thrown in my lap.

Most importantly, running my shop never allowed time to focus on my writing. I've known for years that it's imperative to complete two books I've been working on forever.

And now, the book emerging from these Facebook postings seems like a Very Important Project that never would've occurred.

The message from my pillow dream was also about giving me permission to ask for help and to accept what's given.

I've been the primary person in charge at our shop for twenty years, especially during the December holiday craziness. Since Michael's stroke, many have stepped up to volunteer their help. It's taking courage, but I'm learning to say *yes*.

I've said *yes* to friends offering to bring food to the hospital when I can't leave. I've said *yes* to a crowdfunding site I was encouraged to start, thankfully accepting generous money as it poured in.

I asked for more rehab time for Michael and was told *yes.*

I'm graciously saying *yes* to the generous presence of love being presented to me in so many different forms.

My next challenge is to ask for help doing the things I never had to think about because Michael handled them. Some resistance there, but getting better.

I'm grateful for not only tonight's 'nightmare,' but the one called a stroke that woke me up to one more layer of who I REALLY am: The one who mustered the strength to scream; the one who forced herself awake; the one who didn't allow herself to suffocate.

And the one who's choosing to navigate this life adventure with Michael to learn some Really Big Lessons.

Then again, maybe it's just guilt for sleeping with the two extra pillows I absconded from Michael's bed!

The Whole Truth and Nothin' But

Rolling into our room after two hours of physical therapy, Michael immediately turns on the TV. We relish a few minutes of mindless relaxation before his next session.

Limited channel surfing lands on reruns of the old "I Love Lucy" show.

Watching it religiously as a child, it's just as funny now as then. The simplicity and timeless humor is like a cool glass of water in a moisture deficient, temperature controlled hospital room.

This particular episode has Fred, Ethel and Ricky dare Lucy to spend a day being completely truthful.

Predictably, she's instantly faced with a situation, struggling with how to admit the truth in a "nice way" to a friend. She ends up failing miserably, doing her classic redhead pouty *waaah* of dismay.

Laughing like it's the first time ever seeing it, I start thinking about the many challenges of being truthful.

Most of the time, we tap-dance skillfully around the truth, thinking it's somehow 'nicer' or easier. We do it all the time, justifying, rationalizing, excusing.

But those "reasons" really just boil down to FEAR (False Evidence Appearing Real).

Recently, I had a perfect opportunity to speak honestly to a friend but chose not to. Instead of saying what was *really* going on in me, I 'made nice-nice,' thinking it would be safer and easier.

In other words, I bought into fear.

Next thing I knew, all hell broke loose with this person, leaving my head spinning with confusion.

Whahappened? I wondered, innocently.

I'd gone completely amnesiac about the "little" choice I made that turned this hairball into a full-on relationship choke.

Yikes.

Instead of lovingly, responsibly stating my truth (admitting the real issue, the fear that was triggered) I thought it a better choice to gloss over the situation and not be authentic.

The power of the hidden motive behind the words we speak, always sneaks out, energetically or otherwise.

Fake smiles glued on, we think no one can tell. Our bases (or asses) are covered, but, like a hose turned on full blast, it spurts wildly.

All over the place.

And everything feels really off (and gets really soaked) until the truth is acknowledged.

Watching Michael struggle to get out even the most basic words and simple requests reminds me of the *real* power of communication. As I tell my students, communication is about what lives behind the words, the energy of our *true* intention.

Words are used to cover up an unspoken desire to be heard, understood and acknowledged. They also cover up our *fear* of being heard, understood and acknowledged.

Whenever there was an issue going on in my relationship with Michael, we upheld a firm agreement to talk about it until it resolved.

What that meant was digging deep and determining the *real* issue, beyond what it looked like on the surface.

In other words, an ongoing argument about leaving the toilet seat up undoubtedly had nothing to do with the toilet seat. Even if it appeared that it was.

It took us a while, but we got pretty adept with our shovels, discovering layers to even the most mundane, superficial-appearing "discussions." Even during heated conversations when it would almost be impossible to hear what the other was saying, we plowed through.

Anger tends to put cotton balls in our ears. When Michael used to express something that would push my buttons, his mouth would be moving, but I was so wrapped up in needing to be right, to prove my point, or to get him to just change, I couldn't even hear what he'd just said.

Michael, in his magnificence, would recognize what was going on, stop his talking mid-stream and look me straight in the eye: "You're not hearing me," he'd say calmly.

Although I would want to argue, I knew he was right. So, I would stop, rewind, and ask him to repeat what he'd just said. Once I could really hear his words, I'd look within and get in touch with The Real Issue.

Which never had anything to do with him at all.

It was always all about me. Always.

Now, when he knows exactly what he wants to say but can't get the words out, I'm reminded of the skill I've mastered called *just listening*.

Right now, his needs are simple, but as his brain is re-awakening, they're starting to get more complex.

Like last night.

He was trying desperately to communicate something. He cave-man grunted, uttered a random bunch of jumbled-up syllables, and dove into reciting the days of the week which he'd recently mastered in speech therapy.

None of which expressed what he wanted to get across.

I just assumed he was requesting some sort of physical need since that's what he usually does. So, I rattled off a litany of questions: *Do you have to go to the bathroom? Are you tired? Are you hungry? Are you thirsty?*

"No, no, no. NO!" Anger mounts. His thoughts are clear to him but the words come out incorrectly.

That's what expressive aphasia does.

Usually I'm good at determining his desires, but this latest bout is illusive. His face reddens. His brow scrunches. He keeps trying to squeeze out words that speak his crucial concern.

Since Michael is a pretty deep guy, I decide, what the heck, I'll go more conceptual. Intuitively I figure out exactly what's going on.

"Are you frustrated?" I asked gently, not wanting to put words into his mouth, but knowing that, for right now I need to. Like helping a child who doesn't yet have the vocabulary for what they're feeling or needing.

Bingo.

He nods his head up and down excitedly, lets out a sigh, and grabs my hand in gratitude.

"Yes, I get it." I lovingly stroke a cheek that desperately needs   to be shaved.

And, that's all he needs to say.

Yes, the "truth sets us free," once words are located.

Yes, I plan on telling the truth to the person I was making nice with.

Soon.

Without a single Lucy *waah*.

Change of Filters

Shortly after Michael's stroke, several well-meaning people forewarned that soon, all of his "filters" would be gone.

Wasn't too concerned since he couldn't get much more filter-less based on how authentic he already is. With everyone, everywhere, all the time.

But, I heeded the warnings, waited with bated breath to see what would transpire in his already pretense-free personality.

Besides the Chippendales-esque lack of hospital modesty,

his unconcern with who he performs bodily functions in front

of, doing a When Harry Met Sally restaurant scene imitation in the bathroom, and a newly discovered penchant for singing at the top of his lungs wheeling down the hall – nothing much

has changed.

Concern about filters is seriously ironic, since one of the things

I regularly teach is the importance of being real.

As far as I'm concerned, being authentic is one of the most imperative things we can ever accomplish in life. I've actually compiled an itemized "Death Bed Checklist" -- things we will undoubtedly be looking back on at our end of life, either regretfully or with contentment.

Such as: *Did I fulfill my unique purpose in being here? Did I love, really love, and allow love to be received? Did I forgive? Did I serve others in some way?* And, most importantly: *Was I real?*

Sorry, there's no cheating on this final exam. And, I'm sure you can guess what happens if it's not passed, especially if you   believe in reincarnation!

We start perfecting the art of being phony upon arrival. Early   on, we make fear-based choices as to who, and how, we have to BE. In our family, in relationships, in our community, in the world.

"How should I act to make sure I'm loved?" becomes our subconsciously entrenched M.O.

Because these choices are fear-based, we end up living a lie and don't even realize it. Like being an actor on stage forgetting we signed on for the role, we recite the same lines repeatedly   to an audience that's long ago left the theater.

And we stopped getting a paycheck.

The problem is, we're usually not conscious of being "in acts" since they're layered so deeply within us. Plus, we've bought into them so completely, we utterly believe that's who we are.

But, the good news is, with mindfulness we can take off those false-self masks and make other choices. It's hard to be in an act with consciousness.

Or, to say that in a more positive way, it's much easier to be authentic with consciousness.

When I started to be aware of some my own acts, it was quite the wake-up call, an alarm clock going off with no snooze button.

The first one I noticed was my "Needing To Be Cute" act. That recognition felt like I'd been stripped naked to the world, red-faced, caught in the act, as the saying goes.

I thought, *oh crap, does everyone see that about me? Am I the only one I'm fooling?*

I figured that everyone is so involved in their own acts, they probably could care less about seeing through mine. Made me feel better.

So, why is it so scary to just be ourselves?

There's a part of us that absolutely believes we get to control and/or avoid all kinds of things by behaving certain ways.

Less will be expected of me if I act helpless. No one will hurt me if I act really nice all the time. Everyone will notice and love me if I'm the martyr taking care of everyone or saving the world.

My Cute Act allowed me to get away with all kinds of things.
Like not having to work really hard in school. Or not
establishing deep level connections. Or having to really
acknowledge (or feel)   my negative emotions.

Admittedly, that act even reared its head (for just a New
York minute) when I was learning to take care of my post
stroke husband.

"Oh, geez, he better be walking before we leave the hospital
so I won't have to actually be transferring him from a
wheelchair!"

(By the way, I'm officially cleared to do this on my own now
and, believe it or not, it's actually fun! Well, anything is fun
with Michael!)

Some acts we are in may seem positive, but since they are
chosen from fearful, needy places before our logical minds
were more in charge, ultimately they aren't.

Choices made that way ultimately backfire.

How? By keeping us stuck, not remembering who we *really*
are, not being in our power, and not coming from authentic
love.

In other words, being real.

How could abandoning ourselves NOT backfire?

How could living a lie NOT backfire? The subconscious guilt alone is doing us in.

So, those dire warnings about the demise of Michael's filtering devices sound like blessings in disguise to me.

Thrilling, actually.

How sad that it could take having a stroke to help us do what we should be aiming to do every day of our life: BE REAL.

Since Michael was already so close to being an act-less pre-stroke, that's one skill he won't have to re-learn.

Well, maybe just toning down his now highly flamboyant burps?

As John Lennon so aptly reminds in Our Song: "Love IS real."

He also says "Just give me some truth. All I need is the truth."

Being Led by My Nose

Living most of the time from a very trusting place, those more "left-brained" in my life perceive it as being naïve, or even Pollyanna-esque. They find some things I do outrageous, but knowing that *things always work out somehow,* I rarely if ever spend time worrying.

I aim to always follow my strong intuitive sensings, especially when receiving inner guidance from sources that feel like Higher Level Wisdom.

When I feel a strong pull to do something and have no idea why; when someone says something and it stays reverberating in my head; or when something just desperately wants to pop out of my mouth, I've learned to trust. Not always easy, but my attitude is: *Okay, here we go!*

And I go for it.

If I don't, I get to find out quickly, and often dramatically, why I should've trusted.

Needless to say, I've repeatedly had to learn by the pie-in-the-face method, retrospectively understanding why I shoulda listened. It makes it easier the next time to listen.

Sometimes.

Those same left-brainers refer to this lifestyle as 'living on the edge,' 'being irresponsible,' 'not thinking through' etc. But the way things fall into place, tugging me along, it's as though I have no other choice.

When I get to where I've been yanked, it all makes sense. There's clarity, an understanding of why everything had to happen exactly as it did. The Divine Perfect Timing of it all never ceases to flabbergast.

I'm making it sound easy, but honestly, it's been one of my toughest life lessons.

During these last weeks in outpatient rehab, my logical, responsible mind keeps thinking I should be doing more to prepare for Michael's homecoming.

After all, we only have limited time here.

What the hell am I going to do?

Can I really handle all this?

And what about our future? Should I close or sell our shop?

The whirling doesn't last long when I remember that I'm being led, right now, exactly where I'm supposed to be, doing exactly what I'm supposed to be doing.

This moment is the only focus needed.

Easy to get caught up in overwhelm, but, like everything else in my life, I'm never given more than I can handle. May not feel like it in the swirl, but this is one cliché I firmly believe, especially when I doubt that I can.

I trust that I will know exactly what to do.

Okay yes, all of that's true, but I sure would like a clear sign, Universe! Anybody out there? Hello?

Fun, Fun, Fun!

No matter how mushy Michael's brain is, his sense of humor is still in front position.

Sitting in speech therapy, he's being his usual goofy self. Instead of mimicking words precisely as the therapist says them, he puts on an affected British accent! We're all laughing hysterically as Michael makes it impossible to stick to the lesson plan.

Maybe his next career is an aphasiac stand-up comedian?

"You know, people who are able to laugh through all this seem to recover faster. They're able to roll with the punches and not get stuck in depression and hopelessness. Humor really does heal," Randy explains.

Undoubtedly for my benefit.

Well, if that's true then he will be flying soon.

Next, off we go to his PT appointment.

They have a four-step practice staircase in the treatment room. Michael is assigned two therapists to help him re-learn walking up and down stairs.

It's scary steep even for us able-bodied.

Although he's pretty much mastered the one large step he will need to get into our house, PT wants him to practice walking down stairs.

Something he will never have to do at our home, but good to have in his tool box for other future locations.

Our eyes meet and we share a terror-stricken moment. Knowing I need to get past my own panic, be strong, trust the therapists and give encouragement, I assure him that *"You can do it, Michael!"*

Mustering up my most encouraging voice, I take it further: *"After all, Michael, there are three gorgeous women here ready to catch you if you fall!"*

Without hesitation, Michael looks around, feigning confusion, and clearly, out pops the word *"Where?"* perfectly timed.

We all fall out laughing.

He makes it to the top of the stairs and back down. Without needing anyone to catch him. Not that we couldn't, mind you!

Yours, Mine, Ours

This stroke experience is driving home my spiritual teachings in deeper, authentic life ways.

This morning I woke up with a line from a song humming insistently in my head. The lyrics are *"You've got your troubles, I've got mine."*

Asking Google, it reminds me that song was by The Fortunes, circa 1965. Made it to number two on the Top Ten Billboard Chart (do they still use that?).

Haven't thought about that song in forever, actually never cared for it. But, like a scratched 45, it plays in my head over and over all morning.

Prying Michael out of bed for his always-on-time 8:00 a.m. breakfast (he is definitely NOT a morning person!), he spontaneously belts out an astonishing rendition of *"Nobody knows the troubles I've seen!"* Singing dramatically in baritone, garbled, Michaelspeak, it's unmistakably that song.

We jam a few minutes, loudly singing each of our common-themed songs, giggling like the kids we've lately become.

Since everything that happens in this hospital is giving loud and clear reminder messages, what are these songs trying to tell us?

Whenever I post these journal entries on Facebook, I get frequent comments filled with amazement at what I'm doing to help Michael. I want to acknowledge two things:

145

One, when you love someone there's no question that you will do anything for them. Without a second thought.

Two, I'm not sure who's being helped more, me or him. Really.

For over two decades, I've taught a teacher training course where I instruct my students how to effectively and lovingly assist others. One thing I emphasize is how to put aside personal issues and be fully present for whoever they are working with.

It's often challenging since we're so caught up in our own "stuff," believing it's impossible to just shelve it for a while.

There's a lot of interesting things that occur from doing that, but the most significant (and albeit miraculous) is our own "troubles" seem to lift. Or at least the drama and intensity diminishes and things get put into perspective.

This past Saturday at Michael's occupational therapy session, I saw this phenomenon in action. His therapist, a very upfront, pull no punches kinda gal, admitted she was a bit 'under the weather.' We couldn't tell at all, and his hour was as magnificent as it always is with her.

Asking today how she's feeling, she discloses that, even with sleeping the entire Sunday, she doesn't feel much better. Again, her session is flawless, her energy fully there for Michael. 100%.

Michael used to experience the same phenomena when he was exhausted or even a bit sickish when working on one of his massage therapy clients.

Being the concerned wife, I'd always ask if he was sure about not cancelling the session. He would assure me he'd be fine. Invariably, after doing his amazing healing bodywork on them, he'd arrive home absolutely energized, free of whatever illness that had been brewing.

Part of this is the Universe offering absolute support when we keep our commitments to support others.

However, there's something empowering about service, being in the pure energy of giving that ultimately gives healing to the server.

Since it would happen so predictably, I would no longer be concerned about being able to teach when in a personal turmoil of any kind. I'd learn how to put my issues to the side and let my words flow.

And flow they would.

The other marvel is that, whatever issue I had going on, I would attract others going through the same (or similar) concern.

As I opened intuitively to whatever words I was 'supposed to' say to assist them, those words concurrently helped me.

Occasionally I'd get blown away by the synchronicity, shocked at what that "wise person" in me was saying. I'd listen to the words pouring out and hearing precisely what I needed to hear for myself from myself.

Mutual benefits.

Now, I mostly just accept that this is how the Universe works.

Although 'your troubles and mine' may look different, because we're all interconnected in oneness, they are all yours, mine and ours.

So, I guess we might as well just sing!

Never. Give. Up.

You probably knew this would happen. Eventually.

Maybe you were placing bets on when.

Yep, my positivity has left the building.

Spent most of the day freaking out (yes, gave myself permission to), wondering what the hell I'm going to do now.

What the hell am I going to do now???

It's funny (more like ironic), about six months ago, during the thick (or should I say thin) of the worst year of retail sales at our shop, I declared to Michael: *"I'm giving it to the end of the year to see if we should stay open. If we don't at least catch up by December 31, we are done. I just can't do this anymore."*

I even entered a note in my calendar to remind me. In case I forgot.

Should've known the Universe has a wacky sense of humor.

So today, when I get an unsettling text from my assistant who's been completely in charge of our shop since November 24th, I lose it, internally.

Not one to disguise fears very well, it doesn't work. Michael immediately senses something's going on and asks what's wrong.

I can't hold back.

Tearfully, I tell him far more than I probably should, and he takes it hard.

Usually, even with aphasia, people are able to understand what's being said. He completely understands everything I'm saying.

Right in the middle of my meltdown, in walks his speech therapist for his next session. She takes one look at us and realizes something's going on. My Rudolph-red nose is probably the give-away.

"Are you okay?" she asks, since Michael's usual exuberance is markedly missing.

Again, I can't hold back, and sob out my story to this relative stranger.

Without detail, I bottom line: "I think the reality of our situation has hit and I'm feeling totally lost," I explain. "I just don't know what to do. Or what I'm supposed to do."

With patience and compassion, she lets me get it all out. Michael sits quietly, head drooping.

By the time we wheel to her office and start the session, I feel better having expressed so much. However, she can't get Michael to even try to say a word or focus on her questions.

Casually, she puts her papers away, looks at him intently and asks what's going on.

His head slinks to the table. Silence.

Oh crap. Now I've ruined his session.

So, I jump in and start asking questions. "Did what I say earlier upset you?" He nods yes.

"Are you sad?" No.

"Are you angry?" No.

"Are you confused?" No.

"Are you frustrated?" No.

Some mangled words come out that neither of us can translate. Speech therapist, more fluent in 'strokespeak,' immediately determines what Michael is feeling.

"Are you feeling helpless that you can't help Royce?"

A decisive head nodding yes.

I go to his side, hug him as tight as I can and we both cry together.

I assure him that "....everything's going to be okay. We have a lot of people who love us and care about us. But the only thing that's important to me is you getting better. I don't care if you ever walk again, or if we close our store, but I want your words back. That's all."

Once all that is acknowledged, he's able to focus on his therapy and makes even more amazing strides.

Most of my adult life I've followed the directional pull of my intuition, always being led in the most magical ways.

Admittedly, sometimes down some scary corridors, but they always open to extraordinary results.
Often in the most unexpected ways.

If I choose to not to listen to those intuitive, relentless tugs, everything goes awry in my life. Sure keeps me on the straight and arrow (or curved and dangerous, as the case may be), but not always the easiest of routes.

But I can handle anything the Universe throws my way, right?

My biggest being-led-by-the-nose adventure was opening my shop/gallery twenty years ago. It was one of those crystal clear moments of knowing I just needed to do this, no logic, just trust.

Although t's been the biggest challenge of my life and continues to be, I have no regrets.

In this current state of uncertainty, and not having Michael's words to bounce off, I do what I do best: Surrender.

I send an earnest plea to the Universe to please show me what to do. What direction to take. *What's next, please.*

Within minutes after speech therapy, my answer arrives, in an unlikely way.
We roll into the waiting room for his dental appointment. Sitting next to us in a motorized wheelchair is a beautiful young woman.

I'd seen her several times previously at various hospital events, volunteering her time as a 'peer mentor.' She smiles at me and we strike up a conversation. Within minutes, she openly relays her story.

She had a stroke when she was eleven years old and didn't walk or speak for three years afterwards. She looks about twenty five; blond ringlet curls surround her face that glows like an angel.

Her life is simple, she explains, lives on her own with just a puppy. She knows how important it is to give back to the place that helped her get her life back.

After about ten minutes of chatting, the receptionist lets her know the dentist is ready. As she wheels off, she turns around and looks directly at Michael.
Like God speaking through her, she says passionately: "Don't ever give up!" In case I didn't hear, she repeats those four words emphatically.

"Don't ever give up!"

I hear.

Really hear.

A cellular knowing that is the answer to my earlier request, I decide to sit in that enigmatic answer, allowing myself to trust whatever unfolds.

All I can do, really. Now or in every part of life.

Although I'm not sure what steps to take, like Michael, I'm putting all my energy into just (re)learning to walk. One step at a time. And never, ever give up.

Getting a Point Across

Today is about making sure Michael only uses words. No more grunts, mumbles, grumbles or ummms to communicate. No more snapping, pointing and giving me The Look.

Even though I usually know exactly what he wants or needs, his speech therapist emphasizes: *Words, words, words.*

No matter how frustrating it might get.

Now, when he wants something, he's supposed to say "I want.... ." and fill in the blank. It takes several tries, but eventually he figures out the word for his request. Usually with some coaching, sounding of the first letter and lots of repetition.

Or he uses a reasonable facsimile, like this afternoon.

It's shortly after lunch. Michael relaxes in his wheelchair between physical therapy and speech therapy sessions, binge watching more episodes of the I Love Lucy Show.

He looks over at me and starts composing a faltering sentence. I listen hard. His face is serious and focused as he starts again and again until he knows it's the correct words he's searching for.

What comes out is surprisingly clear and emerges fairly quickly, which is still unusual and exciting.

"I want to go..." slight pause, thinks for a moment, and out pops a perfectly formed "ASS-HOLE!" with the same emphasis the baby had when taught that word in "Meet the Fockers!" (If you haven't seen the film, google that classic, hysterical scene!)

"Did you just say *asshole*?" I ask.
A goofy faced "yes" from Michael confirms I not only heard it correctly, but he deliberately chose it.

To be funny.

As I wheel him into the bathroom, I'm laughing so hard I almost pee in my own pants!

It certainly gets his point across! And, his speech therapist loves the story!

All Growed Up

I let Michael sleep in as late as possible since he's so not a morning person. I go to the bathroom, check my emails, brush my teeth and get ready for the day so I can focus strictly on him.

This morning, as I do my multi-tasking ritual, out of the blue, tears well.

Weeping like a child, I'm unexpectedly thinking: "I miss my mom."

My mother died seven years ago.

Although I thought my grieving was complete, apparently there's another layer to be felt. So, I allow the emotions up as I brush my teeth and blow my nose.

Pondering why this sudden burst of sadness, I pose the question to myself. A loud thought hurls in: *You are the adult now.*

Holy shit.

I guess I hadn't realized that, somehow, I'd become the older generation.

And, that I really wish my Mommy was here to take care of all this for me.

Not that she would, but it's a nice fantasy for a moment.

Just Know?

It's the most difficult decision I've ever had to make, but it has to be made: *It's time to close our shop.*

Even though it's the right and necessary choice, the hardest part is feeling I haven't made enough of a difference.

Some cellular need, an inner longing swimming upstream, mouthing: *Did you do all you were supposed to do here? How will you feel at the end of your life? Did you fulfill your divinely-led Purpose?*

Yes, people loved our shop, tearfully convincing me two years ago to re-open after the building we'd been in for 19 years had sold.

Their sincere sadness showed that my original, lofty mission had been fulfilled: *To bring earth-friendly, made with love, soul-nurturing creativity to my corner of the planet, along with authentically caring about each person who came through the door.*

But in my head it's never enough.

Which is the story of my life.

No matter how much I do, how much I give, how much I help people, it always feels like there's so much more I'm *supposed to be* doing. Not because I'm never satisfied or feel insecure about what I do, it's just a Higher Knowing that I'm here to do something -- maybe lots of somethings -- BIG.

That's been a strong inner sensing most of my life, but during this second half, it's the driving force behind everything I do. Absoulutely, each person has a unique and significant purpose on this planet. We all play an integral part in the grand orchestra of life, even if we don't believe we do, even if we feel we haven't accomplished what we are here to do. It doesn't have to be lofty, and it doesn't have to be conscious.

It's just by being here.

Like my Perfect Life Awakening inner transformational courses.

From the minute I uttered my first sentence to a small group of seekers gathered in my living room, I've known that this is my divinely led purpose. My Mission, so to speak.

How did I know? *I just knew.*

Being somewhat of an introvert, along with not believing I had anything important to teach others, it was terrifying. Yet, because of the synchronicity of how it had landed in my lap, admitting that my entire life had been leading me there, I couldn't run.

Trusting became easier.

When I taught, words and concepts would flow spontaneously, most without conscious volition. I *just knew* what I needed to say; answers to student's questions (as well as my own) would come and I *just knew* they were right.

And important.

In big ways.

It took a while, but eventually I stopped questioning what I was doing, why I was doing it, and the perpetual 'why me's' went back into hibernation.

Because teaching felt so guided, with students arriving effortlessly, it was a constant battle between *"Have I reached enough people with this information?"* vs *"I'm reaching exactly who I'm supposed to reach."*

In the last few years, enrollment in my classes dwindled. Dramatically. Not understanding why, I fought it tooth and nail, trying everything I could think of to get more students. After years of struggle, I gave in, relinquishing to what was being reflected to me that maybe I'm done teaching. Closing my office was the final, painful step.

Our shop was an integral part of my bigger mission. After reading the beautiful tributes published in the local papers about our closure, I know that in my soul.

Plus, the opportunity it gave Michael to express his Purpose by tirelessly volunteering to help our small village community, was equally important.

So now, as I close the door on one more aspect of what this life has been about thus far, I trust that what I'll be doing with Michael is just as significant. Being 100% lovingly present for one person or for thousands, spiritually, it's all the same.

I *just know* that.

And, who knows what might show up as I settle into this new role.

Simultaneously, I know I did enough. I made a difference. And I know I will do more.

"So," I remind the Universe, "anytime the next Something Big is ready to show up, I'm ready. I have all the time in the world (as well as some pretty awesome skill sets)!"

Am I afraid of boredom after all these years of busy-ness? *Boredom is really just believing your life has no meaning.*

Decisions, Decisions

Whenever I make a decision and it's the right one, I always feel an instant sense of relief. Finally, I can exhale completely, and I wasn't even aware I was holding my breath.

Finally I psych myself up to talk to my assistant who's been running my shop solo for over two months. She fills me in on the numbers for December. I'm shocked that we are at least 20% lower than last year.

That, as well as so many bills and so many loans, puts us right back where we started from. Zero. And, if that's where we start on January 1, we have nowhere else to go but down.

Numbly, I know it's the right decision, but it's still excruciating.

Honestly, since Michael's stroke, I can't imagine doing what I've been doing for 21 years, the last eight a living recession hell.

Suddenly, it seems so meaningless. Maybe I made up all the meaning I gave our shop all these years.

Maybe I've just shifted priorities.

But what the hell am I going to do? I haven't a clue.

But things always work out. They just do. *When one door closes,* as the saying goes. Well, I'm waiting for the next door to arrive. Maybe it's a window?

All I want to do, for as long as I need to, is help Michael's recovery. That is the only thing that's important. Truly.

First Step: Admitting you are Powerless.

You never realize how out of control your life appears until others not-very-tactfully point it out to you, attempt to prove it with facts, figures and logic.

A few days ago, my sister, an accountant, called my shop assistant and asked her a bunch of questions. Questions she apparently didn't have the nerve to ask me directly.

Like, how is the store REALLY doing?

One thing about my assistant is she's honest. Sometimes brutally.

But she also cares deeply about us, and would do anything to help. As does my sister.

She held nothing back, exposing all the gruesome details. The struggles of the last few years; how far behind we are this year, and, how it doesn't seem feasible to ever catch up as we do every December.

They mutually determined it was time for us to close, something my sister had been advising for the many years of running a non-profitable business.

Logically, I understand her stance, but our shop has always been a labor of love, never about becoming rich. Or, dare I say, breaking even.

We created it purely from a desire to make a difference -- on the planet (only selling eco-merchandise, way before green was fashionable), in our village (supporting local artists and providing shows and events), and providing a healing, soul-nurturing space (spiritual books and uplifting products).

From her strictly business perspective, my CPA sister couldn't ever relate to those altruistic motives because they didn't result in money. Result: We just stopped discussing the shop much. Saved our oft times shaky relationship.

Two days later, hesitantly, my assistant tells me about the conversation. She doesn't hold back.

She's afraid I'll be angry, but honestly, all I feel is relief. We are done. It's over. Time to breathe again: The truth is out.

Even after managing everything by herself during the holiday craziness, she volunteers to handle the store closing. Everything. Politely, I put up a half-assed fight, but she's right: It would be too much for me to bear in person. Plus, my presence would be a distraction to just getting the job done. Which means sell sell sell, not cry cry cry.

First step in healing: Admitting your life is out of control.

Or at least that's how my life looks on the surface.

There's a wise part of me that knows all of this is just the next step in the Grand Design of how everything's supposed to work.

Working out. Leading somewhere. Trusting the process: That's really the first step.

Changing Direction

It takes a day or so, but when I decide to trust what, not only my intuition, but my sister and assistant are telling me, I post an announcement on Facebook that we are closing our store.

Dear Facebook Friends,

Shortly after Michael had his stroke and I admitted to myself how massive it really was, I began pondering, praying and asking the Universe what to do next.

Repeatedly, VERY CLEAR ANSWERS CAME, but it took all this time for those answers to be finally accepted.

Okay, I'm stubborn that way. And it was the toughest choice I've ever had to make so it took a while.

I kept waiting for proof that my intuition was wrong, however, as of right now, I can't deny its accuracy:

IT'S TIME TO CLOSE OUR SHOP.

I know it's the "right time" and the "right choice" because it just feels right. I just know.

Saddens me profoundly because, as you know, our store is not just a store... it's about love, joy, growth, creativity and our contribution to the world in many, many ways.

Very, very, sad, but in-my-bones the right decision.

I'm choosing to see this as just 'changing directions' because truly, that's what it is.

Same purpose, different form. Not sure what that different form will be, but I'm sure it will be revealed.

It was my honor to meet and deeply connect with so many "customers" who I now define as friends. My Facebook posts have shown me even more how much we are cared about.

Please know that you will forever be my family.

Forever.

I love you all and thank you for supporting a trailblazing, greenovative, artsy, soul-nurturing local biz for 21 years. That's quite a run, eh?

I'll be in touch to let you know what unfolds next in my life! Undoubtedly, if it's anything like the last couple of decades, it will prove to be interesting!

The replies, tears and offers of support came flying in the minute I hit "send."

Not unusually, so did tears of my own.

The Two Step

It's a new year and we are here at Rancho still.

The year starts with a bang (not the fireworks kind), having to really practice what I teach. A confrontational conference call from some people who love me, and, even though it was grueling, I experienced it as caring and truly supportive.

And that's all that matters.

Got to clean up some withheld communication, things I should've been upfront about but kept thinking it was just too "embarrassing" and "humiliating" and I would look like a "failure."

All of which I know is not The Truth, but I was temporarily letting fear run my show.

How silly.

Forced or "Chosen"

One of the most important things I teach (and one of the most universally resisted), is that everything in our lives is chosen. Mostly on a subconscious, soul level, but a choice nonetheless.

Our Higher Consciousness is all about personal evolution. Its goal is to get us from fear to love.

What would best cultivate inner growth, awaken us from denial, help resolve fears, learn to let go, be in trust and clean up things we don't even remember doing?

Those are the situations and scenarios that arrive in life, and we can perceive them that way if we choose to. When we do, it everything starts to make sense, and we no longer feel like victims.

I'm getting so much better at sitting in not knowing, surrendering the need for control, and simply trusting. Putting one foot in front of the other even I'm if not sure where I'm going.

Even if I fall flat on my butt occasionally.

The changes resulting from Michael's stroke have only just begun, on every level. And, if my life is at all representative of what many are going through, this past year was preparation
for even bigger, more profound cha-cha-changes.

Now, with Michael as my dance partner and personal guru,

I'm learning to be 100% present, deal with whatever life tosses, remembering how capable I am and cheering every amazing step he takes.

The minute I slip into *futurethink,* everything crumbles.

Including his legs that barely hold him upright.

Although "one step at a time" is clichéd to the max, there is no other way to deal with life. These dramatic life changes that happened from just one momentary event are opening doors, leading us to somewhere even more amazing.

All we can do is choose to enjoy the v e r y slow, one-step dance together.

There's Nothing I'd Rather be Doing

Two days into the new year, I look over at Michael sitting upright in his hospital bed, zombie-eyed, glued to the TV from 8:00 P.M. on.

He looks out of sorts. (Gosh, that's a weird expression.)

I ask, "What's wrong?" knowing he won't be able to answer, but feeling obliged to at least acknowledge that I'm noticing.

He says, "Eh" which in his new language means: "I'm just kinda in a funk."

"Are you feeling blah?" I ask.

"Yesh," he says with his childlike pronunciation.

"Are you bored?" I ask.

"Yesh," he answers.

I sense there's more to it than that.

"Well, we're going to be home in a few days and then you can be bored with me taking care of you!"

He doesn't smile.

Bingo. I know exactly what's going on. He's as terrified as I am to leave the safety of the rehab nest.

"Are you feeling upset about this whole situation in general?"
I ask.

"Yesh," he answers, a sorrowful look clouds his usually goofy face.

Michael is definitely coming out of the permanent Happy Place he's been residing in this past month.

Rather than just listening without comment, my usual M.O., I decide to offer encouragement. "Michael, this is beautiful. There's nothing I'd rather be doing than taking care of you. You are the most important part of my life and, honestly, I've fallen madly in love with you again."

Not that I had ever fallen out of love, but, after almost three decades, the sparkle had dulled a bit.

He looks at me with partial disbelief, partial relief. He has no words to say, literally.

Assuredly, this honeymoon we're on will last forever.

This time.

Crappy Talk, Keep Talkin' Crappy Talk

Today Michael has a different speech therapist since Randy is on vacation. He's had several and they're all great, each with uniquely different style. One is sweet and loving. One gets sucked in by his non-stop humor and they banter back and forth (even without words), laughing hysterically.

Today's reminds me of a no-nonsense kindergarten teacher, speaking v e r y slowly, simple words, extra high decibel level echoing in her tiny treatment room.

His attempts at goofiness are completely ignored; she's on guard for this potentially naughty student to erupt at any minute. Like a teacher trained to work with four year olds, her polished demeanor and specific, commanding tasks offer instant results.

She starts by asking him in a sugary sweet voice if it's okay if they chat a while to get to know one another.

"Yesh," he says.

She asks his name ("Ma nieame is My-cull") he answers proudly.

She asks if he lives in Los Angeles ("yesh").

From across the small round table I quietly shake my head no, differing with his answer. He looks at me in disbelief and says in Michael grunts, "We don't?" We don't. "We used to," I explain, but for the last fourteen years we've lived in the South Bay. He's shocked.

Like, how could we have moved and he didn't know about it? When given multiple choice questions, he usually gets the answers correct. So she tries that tactic: No, we don't live in Northern California, but offering up Southern California as an option, he says yesh.

Then she asks him to point to various parts of his body. This should be a piece-a-cake, one would think. If there's anything my husband knows, it's body parts.

"Point to your nose!" she commands with authority. He has no idea where his nose is. "Point to your ears!" He has no idea where his ears are. "Touch your head!" and his confused expression shows he has no idea what the heck this woman is asking.

Observing this shocks the hell out of me. It feels like one step forward and three steps back.

Why is it that, all day every day, I'm communicating with him, talking about things that are a lot more complex than pointing to a nose. He gets what I'm saying. I know he does.

All I can figure is he's able to understand certain things but not body parts.

Or, maybe Miss Kindergarten Teacher is irritating to him.

He rolls his eyes as she's leaving, something he never does with his other therapists even if they work him hard. All I care about are results, and if her talking to him like a child works, then hey, go for it.

But, he's not a child, knows it, and is annoyed being treated like one.

Back at our room, he shows exasperation when I try to get him to practice the words this therapist just requested. Reminding Michael that it's his homework assignment doesn't help.

When any of his other therapists ask he perform a task, he does it without question. When I ask the same task, he gives me The Look that says, *right, you've gotta be kidding.*

Or he gets angry at me.

Today, he digs in his heals, shakes his head, and says in two of the clearest words as I've heard yet: *"I know!"*

I get it. He does know. And soon his words will catch up. That I know.

And my job is to know that he knows and lovingly be his wife.

So what if he doesn't know where his nose is. Or his ears or head. He knows so much more than that.

Who's the Heck is Carol?

For whatever reason, Michael now calls me Carol. Or at least I think he is. At first I thought he was saying another word like 'careful,' but clearly, that's my new name.

To make light of it, every time he does, I either a) overly dramatize pretending not to hear him; b) make a comment about who is this Carol person anyway; c) remind him of my name and have him say it repeatedly; d) laugh and say, okay George, what do you want? He laughs too.

But, I just want to know, *who the heck is Carol?*

Apparently with aphasia, certain words get "stuck" and, no matter what the person is trying to express, it comes out with that word. *But why Carol? Is there something I should know??*

When his speech therapist attempted to have him re-learn numbers, they would come out as one, three, four, five, always omitting the two. Occasionally he would blurt out four thousand or whatever strange brain link that got triggered.

So, *I shouldn't be snooping through his cell phone for someone named Carol?*

Feeling No Pain

Okay, now this gets filed under Bizarre.

Exactly a year prior to Michael's stroke, I hurt my hip playing a rather wild game of Charades at a friend's house. I was trying to act out the word yoga, and, to demonstrate, went flying down into full lotus position landing hard on a hardwood floor.

Ouch.

It was one of those crazy injuries that just wouldn't stop hurting. My chiropractor worked on it for weeks, assuring me it wasn't a fracture or anything 'serious,' but I was always, *always* in pain.

Especially when I would sit on something hard.

Well, lo and behold, here I am sitting for hours and hours in the rehab hospital, noticing that my hip is absolutely fine. Maybe sleeping on the world's most uncomfortable cot is the cure?

Or maybe focusing on someone else's healing is the fix?

Stages

You know those famous Elizabeth Kubler-Ross stages of grieving that we all supposedly go through, even if we claim we aren't or try to rationalize them away?

I thought I was 'above' that sort of thing, being a spiritual teacher and all. A pretty big rationalization if I've ever heard one.

Like closing a shop birthed from my heart and soul 21 years ago should be no big deal, right?

And having a formerly vital, active, brilliant husband I will now be taking care of full time should be no big deal, right?

And having my entire life turned upside down should be no big deal, right?

Yeah, right.

Stage one: Denial.
This stage has lasted a while. Actually, it comes and goes. Like when I described Michael's stroke as 'mild' even though he was rushed into ICU. And when I thought that, once he gets released from ten days in the hospital, he'd be fine.

Or convincing myself it won't be a big deal once we are home since he's had four weeks of rehab and is doing so much better.

Yeah, right.

Stage Two: Anger.
Haven't felt that one very much yet. This experience is teaching me more than anything ever has, and I'm in constant awe witnessing my heart widening more each day.

Plus, I know that anger is just masked fear, so I can skip that one. Or at least put it aside until it pops up in the future. Maybe it won't?

Stage Three: Bargaining.
Let's change the title of this one to the "If Only" stage, AKA guilt.

If only I had trusted my instincts when I noticed all those 'little things' going on with Michael. *If only* I had insisted that he not eat the way he eats. *If only* I had really listened and memorized all he tried to teach me, all his skills, all the things I now have to do without him. *If only* I had not let one moment pass feeling disconnected from him due to some silly little button being pushed.

Stage Four: Depression.
Sadness, self-pity, feeling lost, helpless, not able to cope. Comes and goes. But, as I said in Stage Two, I see all the miracles every minute and there's not much room for sadness to stick. At least not for too long.

We'll see about this one.

Stage Five: Acceptance.
Maybe all the inner work I've done on letting go, trusting, going with the flow, not resisting, being present, etc. has worked. I feel in acceptance most of the time.

But, if I don't, I know what to do about it. To be continued...
once we get home.

Home Visit

Today two physical therapists and an occupational therapist drove us from the rehab hospital to our home to help make it more "Michael friendly. "

It starts with the challenge of trying to get him out of the car in our very narrow driveway. The overgrown bush preventing the car door from opening all the way doesn't help. No gardening care for almost two months will do that.

Since his wheelchair doesn't move easily on the brick path, the PT says "Let's just walk it!"

Not easy.

His walking is still sketchy. He's aided by a leg brace, a "hemi-walker' (a half walker device for those with use of only one hand, more sturdy than a cane), and PT hanging onto him by the back of his belt for balance. He uses his own legs in a blocking position, ready if needed.

As far as PT is concerned, it's a success. My head spins with insecurities and doubts. How the hell am I ever going to accomplish this by myself?

Carefully observing every nuance, I know they will insist on me doing a "hands on."

Soon.

Like in a few minutes.

No more hiding behind therapists' coat tails. No more living in denial that I'm actually going to be doing this on my own. In two days.

Going through our house with a fine tooth comb, therapists explain where to install grab bars, how to set up a shower bench, and, most importantly, how to get Michael into our teeny tiny bathroom. Quite the feat!

Strange, it's as if Michael has never lived in our house before. In fact, every time his speech therapists had asked him where he lives, he's shocked when I correct his immediate "Los Angeles" answer.

Not that we are crazy about Lomita, but it's where we've hung our hats for years.

The only spark of recognition is when he hobbles into our bedroom. He takes one look at the bed and figures out how to lay down. He lets out a long sigh of relief.

I, too, am counting the minutes to be in our bed again, yearning to snuggle with my husband's good side. (Elephant in the room question: Is there physical intimacy after a stroke? I guess I'll find out soon enough.)

As expected, therapists insist it's my turn to help Michael walk from the living room to the bathroom to the bedroom (a grand total of maybe twenty feet).

We start out awkward (not sure when to help kick his 'weak' leg forward, so he keeps swaying), but eventually we get into the rhythm and it smooths out.

Take a deep breath. Move left leg forward. Not too far. Lean on the hemi-walker. Make sure it's flat. Move it forward. Not too far. Swing hip so right leg moves. Kick his foot if it drags.

Dossie doe! Take a bow! Another dance we've mastered.

Phew, this is quite the workout. Who needs to go to the gym anymore?

Therapists drive us back to the hospital and arrange for any equipment we need. They assure me that I will get the hang of all this.

No big deal, they say.

Trying not to worry.

Feeling terrified.

Something to Look Forward to

"You know," I say casually to Michael as we play our sixth game of Uno in his rehab hospital bed, "I think being your full time caregiver is going to be fun!"

He looks at me quizzically.

I continue: "We've never had time to just do things during the day like go to museums or walk around the block. We won't have to sit at home all day in front of the TV! And, if we want to, we can rent a bunch of movies and do that all day!"

I'm kind of a Type A personality, but hopefully I can be trained.

I hope.

Probably not, but it's nice to fantasize.

It's About Time?

Tomorrow is The Big Day: We are heading home!

Yippee??

Although I was more terrified a week ago before his therapists did their darndest to cram everything down my throat to be prepped, I'm still just a BIT nervous. About a 5 on the hospital pain chart of smiley/frowny faces.

Funny, I've been so focused on what *I'm* going through with Michael, what *I'm* learning, all these great spiritual lessons *I'm* reaping, I haven't really focused on *HIM*, per se, and what *HE* might be going through.

How self-centered!

Interestingly, I noticed shortly after his stroke that Michael had gotten a bit self- centered. Now, if there's one thing this man did *not* used to be is selfish. He's probably the most giving man I've ever met, and one of the primary reasons I chose to marry him.

One of his first post-stroke skills was loudly snapping his fingers. He started out doing it to get my attention since he was non-verbal. Each time he did, I jumped. To his every need. Instantly. Of course. Happy to do so.

However, once he started getting some speech back, I would playfully inform that he needed to 'use his words' when wanting something.

Teasingly I'd say "I'm not your slave;" "Yes sire;" and "Your kingliness desires something?"

I understood that he felt helpless and confused, not able to express what he wanted or needed, so of course he was focused on himself. Who wouldn't be?

But it was so out of character for him. Guessing that strokes affect the personality and levels of empathic caring as well.

One of the signs that the Old Michael is still in there was when he stopped obsessing about himself, looked lovingly over at me, pointed and grunted to a piece of lint in my hair. I leaned over to have him gently remove it.

Sweet and endearing Michael was starting to return.

Tonight is different. Maybe because he's (we) nervous about going home, we get into a full on "argument."

Imagine, for a moment, that he's in bed with a vocabulary of less than 40 words, most of them garbled or difficult for him to retrieve (even if he used them repeatedly five minutes previously).

I had left for a while earlier in the day to drop off a bunch of things at our house. Tonight's nurse, who for some reason irritates the heck out of him, puts him in bed while I'm gone. When I get back, I ask if he brushed his teeth and he says no. He had a tooth pulled this morning and was told to make sure his mouth was clean and rinsed.

Offering to bring him his toothbrush in bed to help clean his mouth, he says a definitive "NO! I can't do that!" Another of his stuck, repeated inappropriately, phrases.

Calmly, I counter with, *of course you can, I'll do it for you.*
Another even stronger negative, irrational response from
Michael.
Irritating Nurse walks in right in the middle of this
interchange and starts adding her authoritative two cents.

"You need to listen to your wife! She's such a wonderful wife
doing all these things for you and you better appreciate her!"

Nice acknowledgment for me, but this stokes his fires even
more.

All three of us start bantering back and forth about brushing
his teeth, nurse in full throttle. After several minutes, she
scowls in frustration and states loudly: "Just let me do it!"

Knowing this won't go over well, I thank her, gently but
firmly explaining I will handle it.

She stomps out, mumbling something to herself. Probably
about what a wuss I'm being.

After she's out of earshot, I ask Michael what's going on.
"What do you want?" I ask calmly, aware that our angry
interchange probably has nothing to do with brushing his
teeth.

Finally, he's able to get his wits about him and points
frantically toward the bathroom.

"Do you need to go to the bathroom?"

"YESH!" he exclaims with a sigh of relief.

"Why didn't you just say *bathroom*," I ask, realizing what a stupid question this is the minute it pops out. He can't retrieve words more often than not, even simple words like bathroom. Pure and simple.

Quickly, we transfer from bed into wheelchair, speedily whisking him into the bathroom (since bodily functions are still difficult for him to control). I'm thankful we've mastered this routine and didn't need Irritating Nurse's help!

Relieved to be relieving, he sits on his throne. I explain that I know it's hard for him to get words out and it's even harder now that there are so many more back in his vocabulary, more options for error.

I apologize for my confusion and he apologizes for losing patience. He takes my hand and gives me his I'm Sorry face.

Unexpectedly, he gets really quiet, puts his head in his hands and starts to cry. Allowing his tears to flow, I ask what's wrong, and he just shakes his head.

These silent words are all too easy to translate: "I'm terrified about going home. My entire life has changed and I don't know what the hell I'm going to do. We're closing our store. I can't do massage anymore. I have no idea what the future holds for us. And I might be this way for the rest of my life!"

So, after I interpret his loud, very clear thoughts into words, he looks up gratefully and nods his head yes.

Being the positive side of the see-saw this time, I self-assuredly explain that he IS going to be fine.

"Michael, every single nurse and every single therapist has told me that you are going to be absolutely fine! You are going to be able to walk. You are going to be able to talk. I know you will. I absolutely know you will. And, I've never lied to you, right?"

Again, he nods his head yes.

We sit in silence, me sitting close by in his wheelchair, him on the toilet. I stroke his arm. I dry his tears.
I can only imagine what he's feeling.

And, as the see-saw flies, I will probably be right where he is when we cross the threshold of our home.

Tomorrow.

Reality Hits (Bites)

If there's a Richter Scale measuring fear, I'm now at a 9.9. If that's the highest it goes.

Not being one who gives in to something as silly as fear (and not like I have a choice), I stop procrastinating, wheel Michael one last time down the long rehab hospital hallway, out the door and into the sweltering January in SoCal day.

Sans therapist, shaking like a _____ (insert appropriate metaphor here), I'm somehow able to transfer him from his wheelchair into our car. Just like the physical therapists repeatedly demonstrated, just a bit bumpier.

Always easier with PT standing there, rectifying any dangerous choices I might make.

At last, sitting in the driver's seat, I breathe a sigh of relief, trying valiantly to get my hands to stop trembling.

Michael sits slightly off center, undoubtedly due to my improper landing skills, but grins in readiness for the next adventure.

A rush of the deepest love I've ever felt for another human being overtakes me as I look at his stroke-erased, innocent, trusting face.

Leaning over to hug him, I'm crazily sobbing and laughing simultaneously. He caresses my hair, a tactic that always calms.

Off we go, zipping through the hospital parking lot a bit too fast, listening to the GPS voice directing how to get onto the freeway. In my daze, I head north instead of south... geez, I've only done this five times these last five weeks.
First-date nervous small talk, I point out landmarks I've noticed on my treks home to shower and do laundry.

"Remember those times I would go home for a couple of hours?" He doesn't remember I ever left.

I relay the harrowing story of the night he was brought by ambulance from his acute care hospital. (He doesn't remember the ride.) "I got totally lost trying to find Rancho in blinding rain," I tell him.

"You would've been laughing hysterically, Michael! Somehow I found the hospital after taking a wrong turn, doubting the directions the GPS was giving me. I was panicking with no idea where the ambulance had taken you, so I started running from building to building in the pouring rain, asking everyone I saw where they bring new patients."

He listens to the entire drama.

"It was a comedy of errors, like losing a child in a crowded mall.

"I kept picturing you laying on a gurney in the ambulance not able to speak and no one knowing what to do with you! I was frantic!

"Do you remember any of that?"

He's listening intently, and says "No." It's as if I'm recounting a story about someone else.

Honestly, I'm glad he doesn't remember. Sometimes nightmares are good to forget.
Unfortunately, I probably won't *ever* forget.

Ready or Not

The thorough hospital staff tried to prepare us for every possible scenario transitioning from the safe womb of professional care to on-our-own independence.

Supposedly I'm an expert at transferring, assisting his walking, and "cleared" to shower him myself.

They even staged a fake fall so he could help himself (and I could hopefully help) recover. If and when he falls. They assured me that *falls happen*, but I'm certain that will *never* happen to us. I'm an expert, after all.

But it's different in the Real World without PT/OT supervision and instant advice.

Or rescuing.

After a forty minute drive home, we pull into our driveway and face our first challenge: Getting him from the car into the house.

The physical therapists had helped him walk our rocky path and take the big step up to the porch. They suggested a wheelchair ramp. Minutes before we left the hospital today, PT presented us with a portable metal ramp they said we could borrow.

"Try it on this curb," he suggested, not giving me a choice. He explained it would be comparable to getting onto our porch.

Even with trepidation, it was relatively easy. Turning the chair backwards, with a running start, whomph, up he goes. Again I thanked whatever part of me had been prepping for this by addictively toning my arm muscles.

However, try as I might, I can't accomplish this task at our porch step.

A running start is the key, and our uneven path, unlike the smooth street recently practiced on, doesn't allow for that.

Crap. What do I do now? Where's PT to save the day?

Walking is the only option.

Michael looks at me with dismay and says one of his mastered sentences: "I don't tink so."

I explain, *It's our only choice.*

He understands, reluctantly. Thank God he's still upbeat.

Remembering everything I'd practiced, I grab his hemi-walker, stabilize him by holding onto the back of his belt, stand on his weak right side for added balance, block his leg with my knees, and, most importantly, pray.

He's wobbly but somewhat strong. A lot stronger than three days previously at our home visit.

Using my own foot, I kick his right foot up the first step as PT had demonstrated. Leaning heavily on the walker, heave, ho: He makes it.

Without giving time to think about it, I instruct him to keep going, one more step, no hesitating.

This is a big one, even for non-physically challenged folks, having tripped on it myself a few times. But, my trooper husband accomplishes it like a pro.

Once inside, we're nervous relief laughing uncontrollably at the comedy of all this. He's breathing hard and very shaky, looking at me with 'what now?' concern in his eyes.

We stand in the doorway to figure it out.

Knowing I can't just walk away, leaving him standing while I get the wheelchair, I panic. Slightly.

"Do you wanna sit here?" I point to our living room swivel chair. An emphatic, grateful *yesh*.

Still propping him up with one hand on his belt, I reach for the chair, turn it toward him, but, as swivel chairs are known to do, it immediately swings back.

Using my knee, I somehow manage to keep it in position, turn him slightly, hold on tightly to his belt and guide him down gently to this soft goal.

Note to self: *Never leave the house again.*

Spent, I slither down to the floor to sit cross-legged at his feet, putting my head on his knee. Eyes close, relieved smile, he relaxes with newfound confidence from hurdles just accomplished. My fears are somewhat appeased, but still trembling from the immensity of what I've taken on.

Several minutes pass. I pull myself up to retrieve his wheelchair that waits patiently outside. He transfers fairly easily, or maybe it just seems that way compared to what we just accomplished.

Adrenalin still pumping, we continue laughing. Kind of hysterically.

Pushing the wheelchair through the house, it's a tight, very tight, squeeze. Flinging furniture out of our path as I navigate, the entire house is immediately askew.

Two tables get shoved into a corner; a hall tree goes away, and an overloaded scarf rack is a definite outa here. Tossing things Willy Nilly into our granddaughter's bedroom since there's nowhere else to put them.

About half way to the bedroom, Michael motions to the bathroom. Ten minutes at home and already my second biggest dread arrives.

Okay, gotta figure it out. Inescapable.

If I take the wheelchair all the way to the doorway, I can support him and sidestep in. But there's nothing to grab onto and the door has to close for both of us to get all the way in.

Still needing my full support, where will I stand when he's sidestepping?

PT mentioned something about this challenge, but for the life of me I can't remember his easy-sounding solution.

"Are you absolutely sure you have to go?" I ask, wishfully thinking maybe it's a false alarm. He still has them frequently as he re-adjusts to bodily signals.

"No, *bafroom!*" he repeats unequivocally.

Okay, let's figure it out.
Pushing his wheelchair close to the entry, I help him up and we start doing a balancing dance. Instinct takes over. Diving under his arm, I grab the back of his pants, somehow help him turn and down he goes.

Plop. Onto the porcelain target.

Another small victory!
While he sits there, I venture to the kitchen to determine what to make for dinner. The expression 'the cupboard is bare' couldn't be more accurate.

Didn't someone volunteer to bring us dinner tonight?

Swallowing any semblance of pride, I send off a text to her. Her instant reply is *no, sorry, not able to do that tonight.*

Crap. What the hell am I going to do? I can't leave him to go to the market and I'm sure not going to try getting him back into the car.

Trapped. Hungry. Exhausted. Delivery food?

A minute later my phone beeps.

Another dear friend, without prompt, texts to let me know she's dropping off dinner. Amazing, miraculous timing for sure.
Maybe I can trust that we ARE being supported on every level.

Minutes later, another angel friend arrives with grab bars and a drill. He effortlessly puts them up in our bathroom.

Telling him about our previous struggle just getting in, he suggests reversing the bathroom door. He does this in minutes. Smart solution. Another miracle.

Wasn't sure we'd ever be able to dance our way into our tiny bathroom again.

My phone beeps again. It's my friend letting me know food is dropped off on our porch. Intuitively, she knew not a good time for a visit.

Maneuvering Michael's wheelchair into the bedroom, I scrape the door jam, the wall and the corner of the bed. Oh well.

I set up a tray for him in front of the TV.

Offering food to our carpenter friend, the three of us eat silently, two on our king-size bed, one in his wheelchair. Like a slumber party.

After he leaves, I clean up a thick layer of dust in the shower from drilling through tiles, wash the dishes, start a load of laundry, unpack two suitcases from the six week stay at rehab, check emails, take out the trash, sweep my neglected house.

Michael sits blissfully watching a month of shows taped on our DVR, unable to figure out how to use our more-complicated-than-the-hospital's remote.

Undoubtedly that synapse will soon re-awaken.

Still sitting safely in his wheelchair, I get his pajamas on him like OT taught us, weak side first.   I bring in his toothbrush and two cups, one with water, one to spit in.
Ready for the next challenge: Getting him into bed.

Thirty minutes of struggle repositioning body and pillows, he's finally in. Just right.

There's got to be an easier way. We'll figure it out.

Soon, hopefully.
I brush my own teeth (at the sink), get into my PJs (standing) and crawl into bed (easily) next to my husband.

Nestling my head on his chest, I exhale with exhausted relief, and snuggle as close as I can without crushing his limp, unmovable right arm.

For the past six weeks I've fantasized being able to just feel my body next to his. Like an addict getting a long awaited fix, I relax.

We are finally really home. Life is good.

Now what?

Why Am I Doing This, Really?

Just when resting on laurels has you thinking there are no more Life Lessons you can *possibly* learn, life throws you a Pop Quiz: Your husband, best friend and business partner has a stroke.

Today's understatement, sarcastic cliché: *What a learning experience this is/has been!*

On every level: Physical, mental, emotional and spiritual. The lessons are doled out equally on each plate, however, being a spiritual teacher, my focus is more on those pesky *spiritual* ones.

Like this current one: *Are my motives pure in choosing to become Michael's full-time caregiver?*

If I only had a dollar for every time I would ask one of my students to "check their motives." Why emphasize that? If what you're doing isn't coming from a "pure" place, results backfire in some way.

So, what's a *pure motive*?

It's when what you're doing has no hidden agendas. Like *gee, aren't I wonderful for doing this.* Or *wow, look at how selfless I'm being.* Or, *poor me, I'm such a martyr sacrificing my life for my husband's healing.*

Little things like that.

Most often, these subtle notions are firmly packed away in our subconscious mind (AKA denial), noticed only when we start getting angry or irritated for 'no apparent reason.' Or feel annoyed doing what we signed on to do. Or guiltily or from a place of duty, choose to keep said commitment, feeling stuck.

Most importantly, having impure motives turns into anger at self, which then turn into anger at others.

A squeaky clean motive means there's nothing underneath what you're choosing to do except unconditional love.

The litmus test is this: *If no one ever found out what you did, and it was never acknowledged in any way, would you be okay with that?*

Like scattering hundred dollar bills anonymously for strangers to find. Or putting money in someone's parking meter and ducking around the corner. Or leaving dinner at someone's door who just got out of the hospital.

Most of the time, when we're being brutally honest with ourselves, the answer is no.

Okay, so here's my brutally honest confession: Signing on as Michael's full time caregiver was made with a few starry-eyed, and admittedly impure, probably unreasonable expectations.

Like: Soon, because of my amazing loving help, Michael will be throwing off his leg brace, tossing his wheelchair, and we will be back to long, nightly, in full sentences, discussions. How wonderful it will be for him to have my special caring!

Like other choices I've made while looking through thick-lensed, rose colored glasses (like, ahem, opening a retail shop...), it's gotten clear quite fast that those were romanticized, exaggerated, idealistic notions.

Just a tad.

So, I pull out my handy inner shovel and begin digging, aiming to discover any other impure motives lurking around the shadows of my choice.

The clue I can't ignore is feeling an occasional, ever-so-slight twinge of resentment while taking care of him.

Like getting a bit edgy when he needs me to wipe his butt *("Really, Michael, I'm sure you can do it! Just try!")*; irritated when he doesn't show gratitude for something I did *("You could at least say thank you for making you three meals today!")*; overreacting angrily at the littlest of things *("I can't believe how long it takes you to just get into bed!")*.

Like today.

Even with the bathroom door now installed the other direction, it's still a struggle dance getting in and out. His wheelchair doesn't fit, so he has to walk about three feet using his walker.

Michael's right leg is very unsteady, and he's not in a great position to get back in his wheelchair. My role is to steady him with my left hand holding his belt and my other hand grasping his pants in front. Simultaneously, I'm blocking his weak leg with both my knees as he prepares to pivot and land on the chair.

Instead of safely steadying himself, he decides to just lunge for the chair, almost toppling me in the process.
Rather than calmly reminding him of the correct way of getting into his chair, I snap. Granted, it's important that he remembers his new limitations (we both forget), but my anger is extreme.

How ridiculous, I think. As ridiculous as feeling angry that a baby needs changing or a toddler needs help learning to walk.

Or a disabled husband needs me to wipe his poopy butt.

I ponder the lengthy list of what it takes to actually get going in the morning now. Our new routine takes about two and a half hours that includes getting up, getting into the bathroom, going potty, taking blood pressure, checking blood sugar, brushing teeth, washing, brushing hair, putting on leg brace and shoes, getting dressed, making breakfast, eating breakfast (he's the world's slowest eater and even slower post stroke), going potty yet again and cleaning up the kitchen. This list does NOT include taking a shower (haven't had the nerve to tackle that one yet!)

With this itemized clarity, I notice some resentful 'tude:

Oh my God, how am I ever going to have a life if this is all I do every day? Will I ever be able to leave him if and when I get a job? What about ever doing something fun again?"

Two months ago, pre-stroke, my life was intense, packed with at least sixteen hours of work each day with teaching and running a shop. Not including our late night "bed meetings," throwing creative ideas around, planning well into the night.

My out-of-character, rearing ugly head reactions, are blatant clues that maybe I have some impure motives going on. *What could they possibly be?*

Another embarrassed confessional gulp.

Part of me wants the world to say *wow, look at Royce, isn't she The Martyr, sacrificing her life to take care of her poor husband. Isn't she strong? Isn't she selfless? Isn't she just so incredibly loving to close her store just to help him?* (Time to write my Woman of the Year acceptance speech!) ICK. YUCK. BLECH. BARF.

The good news is that, once you notice and acknowledge those manipulative, attention starved motives, things can shift.

Why?

Because they aren't who you really are, just a small aspect of your fear-based consciousness that I refer to as the Lower Self.

Or, more accurately, mine.

I'm grateful for those clues, and even more grateful for Michael, my instant and persistent mirror, who recognizes when I'm not being pure (like when I refer to myself as his Personal Slave!) and quickly demonstrates in Perfect ways.

Like refusing to even *try* to wipe his own butt.

Okay, this one has to change. Pure motives. Really.

Secrets, Lies and Chocolate Bunnies

One of the first things we did when settling back home was to catch up on one of our favorite shows – "Restaurant Impossible." Chef Robert Irvine goes into a failing restaurant, and, in just two days, with a budget of $10,000, transforms it completely.

Besides the unbelievable job of remodeling some really scuzzy interiors and improving horrendous food (disgusted, he often spits out mouthfuls on camera), his more important task is discovering why said restaurant is faltering.

Being as much therapist as chef, it's fascinating to observe how he gets to the core of what's really going on. Pretty instantly.

Needless to say, there's always unrecognized issues the owners have, acting out withheld resentments, trying to prove something, family dramas or other subconscious, sabotaging intent.

He's the Barbara Walters of food shows, using his version of tough love to breakthrough even the most stubborn restaurant owners to inevitable tears. The truth sets them free and, in the end, their restaurant succeeds.

Miraculously.

I heard a startling statistic the other day: People lie (which implies we are lied to) between ten and three hundred times a day!

Crazy, right?

The redeeming fact is, like the inevitable skin eruption after a chocolate bunny binge, eventually truth emerges.

In profound Elvis Speak: *"Truth is like the sun. You can shut it out for a time, but it ain't goin' away."*

Especially when the person you're married to is no longer able to check his email due to a stroke.

While clearing out close to three thousand emails Michael received since being out of commission, I "discovered" some things.

Shocking things.

Like, *who on earth have I been married to for almost thirty years* type of things.

If there's anything (I thought) we both held sacred, it's being truthful with one another. The whole truth. No sugar coating. No dodging. Brutal honesty even if we know it might be hurtful.

We know that "the truth will set us free," so we committed to do that every single day. Rigorously without excuses.

I thought we had been on the same page. No reason to doubt. Especially since Michael can instantly tell, even post stroke, when I'm withholding something.

Although my M.O. is to never outright *lie*, just hold things in. Actually, this happens rarely, since I've learned through tough experience, it just doesn't work. Ever.

I thought I was able to read Michael like a book. Apparently not.

One of the things I teach my students is how to trust their intuition to determine when others are being truthful or untruthful.

It's usually foolproof.

Apparently this is a "Those who can, do; those who can't, teach" awkward moment.

After this email discovery (which, out of courtesy to Michael, I'm not disclosing), the foundation of my marriage starts to moan, a few cracks spontaneously appearing.

Not so much because of the *content* of the emails, but rather the issue of secretiveness and trust.

Although there were a few times in our marriage I would rather have been lied to, my mantra is always "I can handle any admission of truth." Why? Because eventually, with truth running the show, anything is resolvable.

And I do mean A.N.Y.T.H.I.N.G.

What makes the situation even more exasperating is not being able to have a two-way conversation with him about it.

Not one to let a minor challenge like aphasia get in the way, I hesitate, but bring it up anyway. Impossible for me *not* to since Michael, of course, senses something going on immediately.

He gives me that quizzical look that asks *what's going on?*

"No, I'm FINE, really" I insist, but with grunts and gestures, he insists, just as vehemently.

Since I'm well aware of what happens when I try to push down issues, it doesn't take much arm twisting to relent. Blech, I vomit out my email discovery, not caring if he can respond with words.

"So, Michael, I saw something in your emails that really upset me," I explain before it can get further in the festering process.
"I know you can't explain what it's about, but I just need to get this out."

So I do. Tearfully. With a side order of confusion that I realize won't be remedied until he can clarify his end. Certainly there's a reason. Probably a reasonable reason. Hopefully.

Feigned or real, he shrugs his good shoulder and, with a resolute shake of his head, denies it all with a very clear "HUH?"

Persisting in this one-sided conversation is pointless, so I shrug both of my shoulders and, like a hot potato, drop it.

It's guaranteed that the first question I'll ask when he regains speech and mental acuity is: "Please 'splain those mystery emails -- now!"

Meanwhile, time to get out the old Windex for a peek inside to see what his secret-keeping untruths are "mirroring" to me. It must be a doozy given how far the needle is leaning on my Upset Meter.

'Mirroring,' is the term I coined for when someone says or does something that pushes buttons, upsets or irritates us in some way. Our negative reaction is a clear signal that there's an aspect of ourselves being shown ('mirrored') to us. This is a part we try hard to hide in all kinds of 'creative,' usually subconscious ways.

People mirror things we're in deep denial of about ourselves, ways we're pretending to be to cover up how we *believe* we really are. They also reflect whatever we are withholding, things we feel guilty or bad about.

So, why do we *believe* such negative things about ourselves?

When we are quite young, we make decisions about ourselves when we believe we caused pain or loss in some way. Even if we really didn't, the power of those incidents is that we *believe* we did.

Then, a part of us quickly tucks those memories deep inside, literally having us go amnesiac about what we've done.

However, what we decided about ourselves is permanently etched into our subconscious, and we live from those powerfully negative decisions from then on.

Since the primary reason we commit incidents such as those is fear, I call them "Fear-Based Actions." They are the most forcefully programmed events of our lives, more so than when painful things happen *to* us.

What happens from these events is we attract similar (or exact) situations to do to us what we did. Repeatedly. AKA karma.

However, because we've gone into denial about what we did, instead of seeing what we attracted as a perfect way to balance it out, we feel like a victim instead.

It's like chewing a piece of gum, tossing it on the floor, forgetting we tossed it on the floor, turning around, stepping in it, and getting pissed at the jerk who threw that damn gum on the floor!

"Mirrors" are the reminders of what we've done, trying desperately to wake us up to our denial so we can clean up the gum we dropped and stop feeling like victims. Mirrors are always accurate, magnifying every inch of those ever-erupting chocolate bunny zits we try to desperately conceal with makeup.

Or, in my case, some untruth I'm hiding.

The tricky part of mirroring is that sometimes the reflections aren't exact. They often show up indirectly, as symbolic representations or even exaggerated to really get our attention. Mirrors reflect ways we would never describe ourselves because we've covered those parts with various forms of deceptions.

Mirrors accurately reflect what's hidden in the darkest corners of our closets, way under that pile of old clothes waiting to be donated to Goodwill.

Needless to say, discovering and admitting what's being mirrored can be tough. Really tough. We would so much rather be pissed off at others, hording that useless bag of useless items we will never wear again.

I decide to meditate, my go-to technique to discover what's being mirrored. It takes several shovels of diligent digging, but at last I determine what Michael is so graciously reflecting.

Interesting, it has nothing to do with lying, but rather showing me a false belief that "I can't be trusted." I decided that about myself long ago, and now it's showing up in subconsciously believing I can't be trusted to take care of a post-stroke husband.

These notions are never logical, but they are believed on a core, less than conscious level. They are fear-based conclusions we came up with to ultimately *keep others safe from us*.

The prize awarded from facing a mirror is worth the detective work, and much better than biting the head off a chocolate bunny: *We no longer need others reflecting our darkness once we turn the light on, recognizing those false notions and knowing they aren't Truth.*

Once we recognize how we've been pretending to be to cover up what we fear others will find out about us, we can become more of who we *really* are. Or, in my case, a caregiver who can be trusted, not from trying to prove I can, but for real. Even better: We no longer need to be subconsciously "acting out" those beliefs to prove we are right about our negative opinion about ourselves.

Other option: We can stay angry and feel like victims. Forever.

Or wait to hear a confession that may or may not ever happen from a man who can't form words.
Thanks Michael. And Elvis. And Chef Irvine.

And really, I'm about as trustworthy as they come. Just don't put a chocolate bunny in front of me. Chomp.

What if I Knew?

One thing about life is, ultimately, we all have to let go of everyone and everything. No matter how hard we try, everything is temporal.

Built-in planned obsolescence.

Life graciously doles out gifts trying to prep us for inevitable big losses by giving us small ones as practice-tests. Depending on how we deal with little things scurrying off (either gracefully or kicking and screaming), determines how much life continues to remove from our plate.

From the minute we arrive in a physical body, it's our biggest Life Lesson: *Learning to let go gracefully.*

From our very first bite, we're letting go of a meal. Just when we sink comfortably into the couch, thinking we can relax, the battery dies in the remote. Even on our honeymoon, we're getting ready to attend our partner's funeral. The moment a baby lets out his first-arrival cry, he's learning to release this body and move on.

Not being morbid, just truthful.

The question is, if you knew a loss was inevitable, given a specific timeline as to when it would occur, what would you do differently?

Beyond the standard responses of appreciating them more, having more fun, or spending less time bickering, the Bigger Question is: *Would you even choose to be with them?*

More accurately, *if I knew Michael was going to suffer a debilitating stroke, would I have chosen him as my marriage partner?*

I do know what I would've done differently – not wasted a minute distancing myself in any way, looked for mirrors (and admitted them) a lot faster!

Not that I feel guilty for those times I was, shall we say, irritated with him, or wanting to walk out the door during an argument, and sometimes (cheeks turning red) actually doing so.

Marriage. Not all bliss. Especially when one's partner is such a picture-perfect mirror.

I also would've not gotten caught in any ruts, mockingly predicting his every move, not appreciating his magnificence. Especially when spending 24/7 with him as a business partner.

If you knew you had limited time with your partner (or friend, or sibling, or parent), what would you do differently?

If you knew everything in your life was going to do a 180, what changes would you make? Would you see things differently?

Here's my unsolicited advice: *Do them now.*

One thing I know for sure: Even if 29 years ago I'd been given the exact date and time of Michael's stroke, I still would've chosen him. No doubt.

Word Perfect

Part of having Expressive Aphasia is getting stuck repeating words or phrases. For whatever reason, shortly after Michael's stroke, even before re-mastering other words, he started saying: *"I can't do this!"*

Repeating like a broken human record.

No matter how often his Pollyanna Wife counters with "You CAN do this!" since I know the power of putting negative messages 'out there,' he's completely unable to control it. Like Tourette's, this sentence pops out involuntarily, and rarely if ever in context.

In his mind, the words he's trying to say are clear, so he's always shocked when they come out so madcap.

Technically it's called "perseveration" (like persevere), and it's one of the most frustrating part of his stroke recovery.

Like today.

We get home after running several errands (he waited patiently in the car), and the minute he's settled into his wheelchair, he starts pointing outside. Frantically.

Looking out the window, there's nothing to see except our neighbor's house.

"What are you seeing?" I ask. He shakes his head no, emphatically, still pointing outside.

Fifteen minutes later, with lots of head shakes, pointing and several 'I can't do this,' I determine he wants to go somewhere.

"Where do you want to go, Michael?" I ask.

"I can't do this!" is his answer.

At this point, I just ignore his automatic sentence since addressing it gets me nowhere.

"Okay, so is there something you need?"

"Yesh!" he says insistently.

"Okay, so what is it?" He points outside again. "Did I leave something in the car?"

"No!" he says, getting more agitated by the minute.

"Is it something you need to get?"

"Yesh!" he nods, thrilled his dense wife is finally starting to figure out what's so obvious to him.

The above interchange is a radically shortened version of about 45 minutes of bantering back and forth with about a hundred "I can't do this!" thrown in for good measure.

Occasionally, I try to change the subject to no avail. I take breaks just for sanity sake (sweeping, scrubbing, dusting, wow my house is clean now!), but when I do he gets even more upset.

"Is this a matter of life and death?" I finally ask since it seems vital for some reason.

"YESH!"

What could it possibly be, I wonder.
Another litany of questions ensues.

"Does it involve your body?"; "Is it a food?"; "Is it something that costs money?"; "Is it close by?"; "Is it something we've done before?"; "Is it something fun?"; "Is it visiting the girls?"; "Is it at Home Depot?" (I thought for sure I'd hit upon the right answer with that one, his former home away from home!)

My lame attempt at twenty questions gets me nowhere except to find out that yes, it costs money and no it's not something fun.

"Michael, I'm so sorry but I just can't figure out what you want, and besides it's dark out and we aren't going anywhere else tonight."

He gives me a dejected puppy-dog look that would melt any heart.

Except mine right then. I've had it.

Excusing myself, I head to the kitchen (to his utter frustration) to start creating one of my killer vegie lasagnas. Thinking this will surely be a distraction from his mystery obsession, I try involving him in the prep work by having him attempt to cut up an onion. With the use of only one hand, he gets frustrated and wheels himself into the bedroom, crashing at every turn.

TV gets turned on and he sulks pitifully.

After dinner the topic doesn't return, TG! But, first thing this morning, he wheels himself to the front door and it starts up all over again. Same pointing, several dozen *I can't do this*, same inability to get me to comprehend what he wants.

Same frustration. For us both.

"Michael, this is getting more infuriating by the minute. I can't imagine what you can possibly need this badly, but we aren't getting into the car without knowing where we have to go to get it! You need to just let it go and move on!"

Firm statement, no result.

Admittedly, I'm now beyond exasperated. Leaving the room for a minute, I compose myself, remember I'm dealing with a child-like, brain injured person in a bearded man's body.

Head-in-hands, I skulk back to his side. Giving him a big hug, I apologize and explain that this is just as frustrating for me as it is for him and that we really need to work on speech skills so this doesn't happen.

"I'm sowee," he says, and the subject is dropped.

This entire interchange, in an extreme way, is a microcosm of what we all go through in our communication with others. We have something inside that we want someone else to understand. It's perfectly clear to us, and we attempt to get it across to them. Yet sometimes it's like we're speaking gibberish, *they just can't get it*, can't get US.

We say it differently, more emphatically, more simply, using different words, and they still don't get it.

Frustrated, we determine that maybe they're just dense, or not willing to hear, or having a bad day or...!

What I teach my students is that communication is all about our TRUE INTENT. Whatever we *truly* intend is what others get from our words. The real message, the energy behind the words, is what's received.

So, we may be saying *I love you*, but if our underlying intent is *I hate you* (conscious or subconscious), that's what's received.

Which is why communication gets so confusing, or turns into verbal sword fights. With no winners. And lots of blood. And many a divorce.

Yep, accepting responsibility for our communication is a tough concept, but when we're completely honest with ourselves, others' responses mirror our *true* intention accurately.

Barf.

So, pondering Michael's mysterious life or death need, I'm still perplexed. But MY intention is to figure out HIS intention or at least help him clarify it so whatever words he says will be understood.

Even what sounds to me like *I can't do this* gibberish.

Honestly, I'm keeping my fingers crossed that whatever this "life or death" need is completely forgotten by tomorrow.

The Return of Logic!

Clearly, Michael's logical mind is starting to return. Daily, we play Othello and Connect Four until we drop, and he beats me at least half the time.

But just as frequently, he forgets how to play the game even after we've played it dozens of times, with me explaining it just as many.

Using games as therapy is amazing. Here's a man who can't talk, read or write, but masters games of logic almost instantly. Any game that doesn't require adding, reading or information works well. Clearly, I see it waking up his noodle.

Sure need to find some different ones. My own brain needs different stimulation.

The Present of Being Present

Any time I'm not fully present with Michael, he knows it, feels it and reacts. Big time.

Like a child who knows you're saying "Uhhuh, I *love* your new drawing," but aren't really looking at it since it's the 100th drawing they've shown you that day and you are about to scream but have to pretend to be the Good Parent... and then wonder why she's suddenly a melting down, out of control brat.

Michael's technique is to either get really sad or "acts out" in some way. Or does something dramatic like falling.

Luckily, I wake up pretty quick and see what's happening. Once I admit how "not there" I'm being, suddenly he can stop desperately trying to mirror that to me.

Consciousness helps.

Accidents Happen?

A perfect way to welcome Michael's 57th birthday is by having to completely strip our king-size bed down to the mattress and wash four loads of laundry. Your imagination can fill in the grisly details.

Refusing to let that influence the tone of his special day, I laugh it off. Like a child having a bed wetting accident, it upsets him terribly, so I don't make it into an issue.

The last load is done and dried. Suddenly, it dawns on me that for the last couple of years Michael had a few random nighttime accidents. I never put together that his body was giving us clues, trying to tell us something way before his stroke.

Thinking it might be nice to do something other than sit around the house, I decide to run a very simple errand and go from there. Not sure where, but with a couple of hours to kill I'm sure we can figure out something.

Loading Michael into the car, off we drive to do the errand. Halfway there I find out we don't need to do it after all, so I start heading home.

Our house in sight, Michael adamantly says "No, no home!"

"Okay, you don't want to go home. So where do you want to go?" He shrugs his shoulder.

"Do you want to just take a drive?" I suggest.

"Yesh!" So off we go, no goal in mind.

222

What a glorious birthday.

Still so appreciative of time we never had before.

Just being together. Even in silence.

With an unmade bed waiting.

How I Spent Valentine's Day

Just read an interesting article that said, *whether we know it or not, we are all living in the past.*

Yes, like a badly dubbed movie, everything we experience is registered in our brains with a millisecond time delay (which could explain those déjà vu moments).

Add that to how our consciousness lugs around our past imprinted experiences, especially traumatic negative ones, we are rarely "in the present moment" at all.

Thinking about that in terms of my marriage, ever since Michael's stroke, my love for him started bursting at the seams. It just bubbles out, foaming at the mouth like a rabid dog, sometimes randomly, and often inappropriately.

Like making out during our lunch break in the rehab hospital courtyard today.

We've been together for almost half my life, and, of course I love him. But now that our life has done a 180, that love feels different.

It's not the giddy, romantic, head-in-the-clouds, walking-on-air kind of love. It's more like a deep feeling of respect, caring, gratitude and awe.

Yet, a self-imposed question haunts me: Am I loving the Michael of now, or the memory of who he was pre-stroke? Am I just living/loving in the past?

Let me tell you about our recent Valentine's Day. This is the first time in twenty-one years of owning our shop that we aren't crazily working the week before and day of February 14th, our second biggest day of the year.

Despite commercialism and sappiness, V-day has always been my favorite holiday. It felt meaningful helping people express love no matter what form it took. Love was definitely part of my shop's Mission, motivating everything I did, every item sold, all year round.

This year's February 14th, at home with nothing special to do, feels surreal.

Frequently, I catch myself anxiously thinking, *uh-oh, there's something I'm supposed to be doing.* I scratch my head and remember that *no, I don't.*

I just have to BE with Michael.

In jest, just to see his reaction, I remind him what day it is. Still blissfully in his Happy Place, there's not a dollop of guilt about not fulfilling his husbandly duty to buy flowers, candy and a card. Not that I want any of those material things, but it's weird not celebrating in some way.

Especially with all this over-exuberance of love flowing through my veins.

So, I pull out some of the stashed Valentine cards I'd given Michael in the past. They're filled with heart-felt words, open, honest, deep expressions of love. Sentimental but never flowery, they're acknowledgements of how grateful I am to be in such a Real Relationship with someone who totally gets me.

This year I don't even give him a card. Not that he wants one. Or knows the difference.

It makes me think about how difficult it is to let go of those dewy-eyed, romantic notions about a lot of things.

Like when people would walk into my shop, look at me with envy and say "Wow, I would love to own my own shop and be self-employed! It must be soooo much fun!"

I'd always smile politely and, based on my mood, reply: "*If you ever want to know what it's really like to own a shop, give me a call!*" Or something snappy like "*Yeah, but my boss is really a task master and she doesn't even let me take a lunch break!*"

They'd look at me curiously until realizing I was mocking myself. Uncomfortable laughter.

Not that I wanted to discourage anyone from following their passion or living their dream. And not that my words of experience would do anything to alleviate needing to go through that initial romantic stage. No words of logic had dissuaded *me* 21 years ago.

Thankfully.

Our obsessive need for romance is a Big One to let go of. Not that romance isn't fun, but relationships are about so much more.

Like growing and evolving together. Or fulfilling a mutual purpose on this planet. Or discovering more about yourself by seeing and admitting mirrors your partner so graciously reflects to you.

All the time. Negative and positive.

Relationships can also be about changing everything in your life mid-stream, learning to be completely present-in-love with someone brand spanking new. In the same, yet completely different, post-stroke body.

Who needs some corny Valentine card.

Not me.

However, I did buy myself a box of chocolates and thoroughly experienced every single one of them.

Without guilt. Yum!

Never, Ever, Give Up!

Even post stroke with so few accessible words in his repertoire, Michael knows me like no one else.

Feeling bummed tonight, without uttering a word, he just knows.

As I wheel him into the bathroom, he asks with concern in his eyes: "Okay?" (Translation: *"Are you feeling okay? What's going on?"*)

"I'm fine," I reply, lying like a pro.

Two minutes later: "Okay?" (Translation: *"I know you're not. Something's going on. Talk to me!"*)

Pushover that I am, it doesn't take much to unleash the floodgates. "I don't know what the hell I'm doing, Michael. I'm feeling pretty hopeless about everything right now."

Patting my arm, he replies: "I know," he says compassionately. Two more words he's mastered lately.

Tears streaming, I walk out of the bathroom and catch up with several things on my list while he does his business.

Hearing his "Um!" signaling he's done, I go back in to help him up.

As I enter he looks up at me and says "DON'T GIVE UP!" clear as a smog free day. Amazed, I cry even harder. He holds me. I will never forget this moment. Nor will I ever give up.

Nor will he.

My next inner question arises: *How would I be feeling if I knew there was no hope for his improvement? Would I be able to be upbeat-cheerful if I knew there was an ultimate death sentence from this stroke? Or a several year recovery process?*

I'm choosing to hold onto what every "expert" has told me: *He will be fine.* Or, at the very least, *he will be a different version of Michael, but fine.*

It's a long road (ranging from 6 months to several years, according to some), but with focused work and desire, he will be back.

But the question still haunts: *What if he stops making progress and this is how he will be?* In other words: *This is how life will be.*

For me. For him. For us.

Hope is what drives people. Motivates. Keeps us going. Without hope there's nothing.

Yet, just hanging around a-wishin' and a-hopen' weakens us into inaction.

Even deeper, if we don't admit to and address our subconscious *hopelessness,* the part of us that constantly fights wanting to give up, we will be at war with one of our profoundest Core Issues. One that gets constantly triggered, getting in the way of feeling consistent joy, power and meaningfulness.

I find that, once we open the door to feeling our emotions, we start feeling deeper levels of everything. What tags along often unwittingly is feeling our often denied sense of hopelessness.

This can be beyond distressing.
Although we may think it's best to not let hopelessness past our front door, that works in just the opposite way: The more we resist feeling it, the more we end up numbing out to life, aliveness, pleasure, joy, love.

The more we resist our core level of hopelessness, the more it persists.

Also, the reverse is true.

Once we allow ourselves to really, *really* feel our hopelessness (mindfully, not just wallowing in it), we can get to the bottom of it and it's no longer a scary monster we have to block out.

We see it for what it is: Just another emotion.

The reward? It loses its oomph. Meaning we don't drop into a pit hopelessness when scared or angry, or, if we do, it doesn't last long.

Hopelessness might be scary to admit and welcome in cause it's certainly not a pleasant house guest.

Which could be why so many suffer from depression -- we've learned to deny hopelessness, suppress it completely, pretending and acting like everything is fine.
All the time.

No matter what's really going on.

Giving it fertile feeding ground to run amok in.

Where does hopelessness come from?

It's quite the duality. It comes from a false notion that we are unimportant, that our life is meaningless, that our existence is a big waste. Even though all of that is literally impossible. *Just being* is proof that our existence is important in ways we may never understand in the Grand Picture of Life.

I find that one core reason we're prone to hopelessness is because we believe we're not fulfilling our Purpose in being here. That notion gets even stronger every time we withhold who we *really* are. Or ignore what we know we are *supposed* to be doing.

Which, sadly, is so frequent. We simply don't allow ourselves to be authentic or trust our deepest awareness of why we are here.

However, the biggest reason we're prone to hopelessness is from subconscious deservingness issues.

In other words, hopelessness is the downward spiral that gets triggered the minute we choose to buy into fear and not be the magnificent beings we are here to be.

Here's the Big Life Pattern we live out: *"I'm here to be loving, and I chose to do something that wasn't loving... now I'm hopeless and don't deserve (fill in the blank) and I perceive life as hopeless."* The cycle gets stuck, trying ways to resolve it to no avail.

Until we wake up and see what we're doing and why.
Which leads me back to my own feelings of hopelessness.

Do I not believe I can help Michael come back? Do I not trust that there is hope?

Or that I am hope?

A smidge. But mostly I'm in NEVER GIVE UP mode.

We BOTH deserve that Truth.

Our First Fight

Well, it finally happened: The honeymoon is over.

Our first post-stroke fight.

It starts when I insist that Michael walk from the car to the house, something he's been doing for a few weeks now. It really makes a difference in his strength and stamina.

He insists that "I can't do this!" I insist that he can.

"Michael, of course you can. You've been doing that for weeks!"

Eventually, I win, and of course I'm right: He does it. Bitching and moaning and giving me The Look the entire twenty foot walk.

A couple of hours later I remind him that he has homework from his physical therapist: To stand up a few times every hour and to stretch his arm as much as possible.

"I can't do this," his stuck phrase, annoyingly, reappears.

"Of course you can, Michael!" I insist, reminding him how important it is that he exercise and stretch. I even repeat what PT said, word for word, so he knows it's not just coming from me. Sometimes that helps.

"I can't do this!" louder.

I try meeting his protests with logic. "Michael, of course you can! You've been doing it really well for weeks!"

"I can't do this!!!" even louder.

"But why?" I continue, starting to rapidly lose patience.

Several more back and forths. We both reach our breaking point. He yells NO NO NO! and I say YES YES YES just as loudly. Even with more words at my command, I keep it simple.

Furiously, he starts trying to wheel his chair out of the bedroom and into the living room, just like when we would argue in the past and he'd storm out of the room.

Luckily, the path is blocked with far too many things and sharp turns to navigate and he gets stuck.

Laughing at how ridiculous this interchange is doesn't help.

For dramatic effect, I do something I rarely do: Get into bed in a huff, leaving him to fend for himself. Which of course he can't do. So he sits in his own huff, tapping his five usable fingers, glaring.

Best fifteen minutes of sleep I've had in months.

The first to make the move has to be me. I help him get into bed in icy silence. Without saying goodnight.

The next morning he's still sulking.

I already figured out my side of the mirror, so I bring up what happened, calmly explaining why it upset me.

"Michael, when you don't believe me when I tell you that you can do something when I know you can, really pushes my 'I'm Stupid' button. You know, that silly untrue notion I have about myself not knowing."

Even with stroke brain, he remembers hearing me talk about that repetitious issue many times previously.

It's a doozey of a button, goes to my core, and, since it's still pushable, there must be more to look at about it.

Usually at this point he would acknowledge his own issue that had been triggered and we'd be able to laugh at the perfect mirrors we reflect to one another. I can only trust that he's seeing his own mirror silently.

Even if he isn't, we are able to make up.

All is good.

And, his "I can't do this" phase is starting to lessen.

Giving Care

A few weeks at home and we're going a bit stir crazy. I suggest a little field trip to a local mall.

Although neither of us are mall types, a long sigh of relief is followed by a goofy, grateful, grin. "Yesh!" he says as his head nods in excited agreement.

Which is shorthand for: *"It's about time! If I have to play one more game of Connect Four with you I'm going to scream!"*

Or maybe that's what *I'm* saying without words...

An hour of preparation later, making sure he uses the bathroom we've finally mastered, he piles onto his wheelchair. Moving through the now clear pathway, we roll backward down the metal wheelchair ramp. With a great deal more confidence than when we left the hospital, getting into the car is difficult but manageable.

Zooming over ten minutes over to the closest mall, I'm thinking about my favorite vegie burgers served at one of the restaurants there.

It's been a while since I've set foot in a mall. The parking lot is crazy busy, but our new disabled permit allows us to avoid the hassle. I unload his wheelchair and, without much help, he about flies out of the car. Quite an improvement.

Bounding to the entrance, we converge into the real world. First time in two months.

Slight culture shock from the quiet of home into sensory overload, so we decide to eat lunch first. Surprisingly, Michael is able to read the menu and determine exactly what he wants. Didn't realize he could do that.

Lunch done, and before the waitress even clears the table, my biggest fear arrives: Michael has to use the public restroom. Even though he'd gone before we left.

He needs lots of assistance in every area of life, including bathroom duties. Signaling the server with a desperate look, I ask whether they have handicapped restrooms where a caregiver can accompany. Of the opposite sex.

Excusing herself, she goes to ask the manager. From across the restaurant I see him nod yes. "Of course we do, and feel free to use either the men's or ladies room," she reports. Thank God for ADA!

But, which do I choose? Selfishly, I opt for ladies, even with Michael's violent head shaking and loud grunts of protest.

As long as I'm in charge of pushing his wheelchair, there's *no way* I'm ever going into the men's room with him. Really don't want to see a bunch of guys wee-weeing in urinals. Well, maybe it would be an interesting experience, but let's save it for another time.

Hopefully never.

Thankfully, the ladies room is empty. We slither into the large disabled stall and proceed to get him out of his wheelchair and onto the potty. As he relieves himself, I plunk down on his chair, check my email, answer a few texts and wait patiently.

Michael being Michael, he starts making noises and being silly. Firmly, I hush him, afraid of being busted for sneaking a man into this female sanctuary.

He would always get annoyed when I used to divulge this, but he's a really slow guy when it comes to toileting. Post stroke, even slower.

Like a tortoise in molasses slow.

Several shifts of women come in to use the stall next to ours as I sit biding my time, hoping no one hears his man noises. He would never admit this, but I think he's enjoying the cleanliness of a ladies room as well as the furtive idea of being a man in this secret world of powdering noses.

Finished at last, we wait until the coast is clear and high-roll it out.

"Phew, no one even saw us Michael!" I say thankfully.

He looks relieved. In more ways than one.

As we wander looking into three floors of shop windows, I ponder the idea of being a caregiver. This is a role I never thought would've landed in my lap, but honestly, it feels like I've been training for it my entire life.

In my classes I teach the difference between *rescuing* and *assisting*.

Rescuing is when we see in others our own unresolved pain and want to save them (really just trying to save ourselves) from it.

It's feeling bad for someone because we perceive them as a victim, not as a Higher Consciousness Being who has chosen their life path (consciously or unconsciously) for the lessons they are here to learn and/or teach.

Deeper, it's actually feeling bad for *ourselves* for the choices *we've* made rather than seeing, trusting and learning our *own* lessons.

Assisting, on the other hand, is coming from a place of True Caring. It's compassionately trusting people to go through their life journey on their chosen path, learning lessons how they are meant to be learned. Caring enough to know you cannot, nor should you, try to rescue them from their lessons. Even if they seem stuck. Even if they seem lost. Even if they seem unwilling to learn.

Yet, it could also mean holding their hand for a while when they're learning to cross the street, trusting they will be doing it by themselves when ready. Knowing when the time is right to release their hand even if they disagree. Or when you are scared to.

As we jaunt past shop after shop, I realize that being a caregiver literally means GIVING CARE. Showing care. Being care. Expressing care. Taking care of.
How does one care?

By knowing what the other *needs* rather than *wants*.
Trusting their lessons, and letting go with trust when it's time for them to learn for themselves.

Every single day, the privilege of participating in Michael's healing, teaches me more about true caring. And trusting.

And hoping that soon he will be able to go into the men's room by himself. Really.

By the way, at last he's able to wipe his own butt! Small miracles abound!

No Breaks for the Weary

When I told my friends I'd be taking care of Michael full time, a few of them looked at me in amazement.

"You'll go nuts!" was the consensus of opinion.

Given my somewhat Type A Personality (I call it having Big Purposes to fulfill), and how different the direction this fork in the road is taking me, I understand their concerns.

But honestly, every day is filled with things to do, lists to check off, and of course, Michael to attend to.

By the time he wants to go to bed (at an early ten now) I'm ready too. But by then, I have to catch up with everything I need to do, so no rest for me.

When we opened our shop, I had a very romanticized notion about working for myself. Little did I know that being my own boss meant working for a task-master. No breaks. No lunch. No walks on the beach. Sixteen hours a day was our minimum.

Being a full-time caregiver means just about the same thing.

Every night I look back on our day and, although it doesn't seem like we did much, every minute was filled.

And, I feel just as Big Purposeful.

Feel Feel Feel

Several have warned that stroke patients frequently start experiencing intense emotions.

Tonight, Michael blows the lid off his pot of emotions that may've been boiling for a long time. Was this stroke catalyzed, or just time to finally release long-suppressed feelings?

We sit in bed watching the Oscars, enjoying the fashions and clips from the many films we missed seeing this year. In the past, we would pride ourselves on having seen all the movies nominated. Oh well, next year. As always, we laugh at the funny parts and get bored listening to drawn out acceptance speeches.

Someone talks about Glen Campbell who's suffering from Alzheimer's. They introduce a singer who will be covering a song he wrote to his wife. As he sings, out of the blue, Michael starts sobbing.

Not just sniveling, but gut wrenching, child-like, someone-just-died sobs.

We've gone through many losses together. Cats, dogs, rabbits, guinea pigs, both sets of parents, uncles, friends. He's not one who ever holds back tears, cried freely at each death.

But nothing like this.

The sobs are so intense I get concerned. He can't stop.

All I can do is what I've always done: Hold him until it finally quells.

Glad he's able to get out some sadness, even though it seems a bit extreme for the situation. He's not even a Glen Campbell fan.

However, I know it's all sadness from the same pot.

Sure better than anger.

Three Three

Since his discharge early January, Michael and I diligently go to outpatient rehab at Rancho twice a week. He's making V E R Y   S L O W progress, but any progress is good. Really good.

Today, we sit outside in the beautiful pre-spring weather, having lunch between therapy sessions. As we munch on sandwiches, he starts desperately trying to communicate something to me.

Although his vocabulary has increased tremendously these last couple of months, his words are still few and far between. Few   is the operative word. Maybe thirty or so, but who's counting?

Most often he still uses gestures and gibber-grunts to get across what he's trying to say. I've learned to play charades with him until I figure out the word he's aiming for, and, if not, I ask enough questions until I do.

Today is monumentally frustrating.

In mid bite, he gets very upset. "What's going on Michael?" I ask, thinking maybe he's tired of eating the same things I've been fixing for lunch. Every single day.

Admittedly, I'm not the most creative lunch chef even though I obsessively watch Food Network shows.

"Are you upset about something?"

"No," he says.

"Are you afraid?" Another no.

"Are you sad?"

A definitive "Yesh!" accompanied by potential whiplash inducing head bobs.

"Why are you sad?" I query, knowing his thoughts still won't translate into discernable words, but force of habit is hard to break.

He starts saying the word "three" repeatedly. Clearly.

He uses hand gestures, holding up three fingers and then saying three again. Picking up his weak hand, raising its three fingers, saying three again.

"You want three of something?" I ask.

"No!" he replies.

"Is it because I keep giving you the same three items in your lunches?" He thinks for a moment, smiles sardonically and says "Well, no." Phew.

A few more lame questions trigger more needle raises on the no meter. He's getting utterly frustrated at my cluelessness.

This back and forth continues for about twenty minutes until I finally say with exasperation: "Michael, I have no idea what you're trying to tell me! It seems important but I just don't get   it! I'm so sorry! But we need to get to therapy now so let's go."

Crestfallen, his head hangs the entire roll to his session.

Perfect timing: Our appointment is with his speech therapist. She's his best translator, usually able to understand what he's trying to say in strokespeak.

Lately, she's having him parrot sentences.

Unfortunately, they don't "stick" very long out of the therapy environment, but at least he's able to practice with her. Maybe soon they will etch into his still mushy brain.

After a brief greeting, she starts her repartee. "So, Michael, it's a new month. Do you know what month it is?"

I wonder why she's asking that, knowing there's no possible way he will have   the answer. She takes out her white board and starts to write the word March.

Before she even finishes the second angle on the M, he snatches the marker from her hand and shakily writes the word MARCH. "Wow, good job Michael," she gushes.

I don't know who's more impressed, me or her.

"Can you say the word you just wrote?" Words still don't roll off Michael's stroke-strangled tongue, so she generally has to cue him by starting off the first sound.

Remarkably, this time he effortlessly blurts out "March!"

More gushing. From us both.

"Do you know what the date is in March?" I figure now she's really pressing her luck, but out pops "Three!" as though he's been waiting for the teacher to finally ask a question he knows the answer to.

The minute he says the word 'three' it dawns on me: Today is March third. Today is his Dad's birthday. Oh my God, that's what he was frantically trying to tell me at lunch. Three, three! It's one of those "Could've had a V-8" moments.

"Michael, it's your Dad's birthday, isn't it?"

"Yesh!!" he says elatedly. His dense wife finally figures out what's so obvious to him. If he could've said duh, I'm sure he would've.

I can't contain my tears. "I am so, so sorry Michael...that's what you were trying to tell me at lunch with the three-three, right?"

"Yesh!" he says, looking as thankful as relieved.

I explain to his therapist what happened at lunch and how insistent he'd been with the three-three gesturing.

"It's so weird cause I have no idea how he could possibly know it's March third!" I explain, but knowing how important his   Dad was in his life, I'm sure the date is permanently etched in some fold of his brain.

Even post stroke.

Even though his Dad's been gone for over twenty five years.

Now it's etched permanently on my smart phone calendar.

Patience, Patient

When people ask how Michael's doing since his stroke, I never quite know how to answer. Depending on who's asking, my responses range from "He's okay" to "About the same" and a range of at least fifty shades of gray in between.

Most often I comeback with "Well, he's making very slow progress each day" and leave it at that.

Remembering hearing many a proud parent's blow-by-blow (yawn) about Their New Baby, I assume that even my most caring friends probably don't want to hear all the details.

T.M.I. for sure.

On the way home from our twice weekly outpatient sessions, the glowing praise from his speech therapist is still sinking in. She gushed about how far he's come, reminding me how he was just a couple of months ago: Neanderthal grunts and unable to mimic even the simplest of sounds.

She's right, of course, but from this (trying to be patient) vantage point, all I see is me not being able to have even the simplest, how's-the-weather conversation with my husband.

I'm thankful he understands everything, but getting out words from his chunky peanut butter brain is still almost impossible.

Which leads me to my latest True Confession.

Pre-stroke, if you were to survey Michael as to what his wife's Biggest Life's Lesson was, his unabashed and instant response would've been: "To learn patience!"
His eyes would twinkle as he'd throw me under the bus, considering the face I show the world is just the opposite.

An act? No, just impatient with him.

If you asked anyone else, they would swear I was the most patient person on the planet. I could listen to friends rattle on forever about anything without interruption. My students were never pushed, prodded or told to just GET IT already! My motto: "It takes as long as it takes," learned from years of (patient-gaining) experience.

But, as I've reluctantly acknowledged on previous pages, *Michael is always right.*

So, since we are all here with an assigned list of lessons to learn and tests to pass, what more effective way to learn about patience than to be handed a caregiver role for a post-stroke husband.

Even pre-stroke, Michael was beyond slow doing almost everything. I could set my watch for precisely twenty minutes during his bathroom visits. I'd be done eating dinner and have the kitchen completely cleaned up before he was halfway through his plate. Trips to Home Depot for one item would take hours.

Needless to say, he was always (not so fashionably) late. We lovingly coined it "Michael Time."

The common denominator when health professionals discuss stoke prognosis is: *It's a slow process,"* non-committal about even approximate recovery times.

Trying to pin down one of his doctors, I had asked persistently: "So, does slow mean a month, six months, a year, two years?" His white-coated, lack of eye contact response was: "There's just no way to tell, but strokes like Michael's could take two years or so."

It was the "or so" that got me.

I figured, if I couldn't get a straight answer from doctors, maybe peer patients would help. People are very chatty in rehab, so I never hesitate asking specific questions to anyone who has that 'post stroke look.'

I can spot 'em easily now.

Interestingly, every person has the same two things to say: One, *it's a long journey.* Two, *don't give up.*

They always look me straight in the eye, intensely, when they say that, and repeat it just to make sure I get the message.

Yep, I hear it loud and clear.

But then again, one of my life's missions is trying not to buy into other people's "belief systems" since I know they don't need to be MY truth.

Things like "The reality is..." or "You shouldn't open a retail shop without experience..." or "You know, we're in a recession so everything's going downhill..."

It's tougher now since this is regarding a life-and-death situation. It's hard to not blindly accept what 'experts' say as they fill my ears with scientific experiences and show x-rays of exactly what Michael's brain looks like now.

But, I digress. Back to learning about patience.

In my recent hectic life as a shop owner/spiritual teacher, Michael would do anything he could to make sure I'd slow down and smell the roses. (Notice I didn't say stop.)

Like pulling the car over to watch a magnificent over-the-ocean sunset I was missing while answering a text.

Or grabbing me, forcing me to dance around the store with him before we would open... just to raise my energy and make sure I was fully, joyously, present with him. How could that not bring my 'goofy on' and set the tone for the day?

Now-a-days, we take leisurely neighborhood "rolls," an activity we never had time to do previously.

Whenever there's something beautiful to look at or something he wants me to notice, his foot becomes a Fred Flintstone brake, bringing the wheelchair (and me) to a screeching halt. Although I've almost toppled several times, it's worth the trip to pull me into the moment.

Which apparently I still need his help with.

Now that it takes a zillion times longer for him to do every single thing, those patience lessons are in my face minute-by-minute, hour-by-hour, day-by-day.

Like walking the twenty foot distance from our car to the front door that takes close to fifteen minutes; the almost three hour morning readiness routine (sometimes two if I prod. A lot.); or getting a word out that he's spoken his entire life that can take an hour.

The list is endless.

As we continue the forty minute (very quiet) drive home, suddenly I'm mesmerized by trees gracing the sides of the freeway. Trees standing proudly along every street.

Entranced as though I've never noticed these immense plants before, their branches sway, leaves fluttering hello to grab my attention.

Always fascinated with their beauty, I wonder why this sudden, overpowering magnetism.

Vaguely, I remember a meaningful meditation I had years ago about the mystical lessons trees are here to give. Lessons such as: Slow steady growth; have deep roots; be strong through flexibility; branch out; and the inter-connection of life.

Oh, and, that darned patience message.

Without time lapse photography, it may seem like nothing is happening, but every day tree roots grow deeper, branches divide and get stronger, leaves photosynthesize and provide life-affirming oxygen.

Just like Michael, slowly coming back.

Slowly? Yeah. And that's okay because it's a process not a project.

But, really, can I pass this patience test? *Now?*

Outa Control

Shortly after Michael's stroke, it got clear that, no matter what little control of his body and life he actually has, he's going to try to maintain control in any possible way.

That's just how he is. Wouldn't term him all the way into "control freak," but well, let's just say he likes to be in charge.

Sometimes it was a good thing, like planning our vacations to the minute so we never had to frantically look for vacant hotel rooms. Yet, I would've loved not being tied to his inflexible schedule to do some spontaneous, nomadic exploring.

It used to be one of our ongoing battles. Sometimes the Universe would provide opportunities for me to win the battle by throwing unexpected monkey wrenches in his pristine plans. Very upsetting to him; I would be smirking irrepressibly.

Mostly, like a well-trained wife, I'd graciously allow him to *think* he was in charge, knowing who really was.

Today, a few weeks home from the hospital, Michael's has a bit of a fall while taking the one step down from our porch.

As always, I'm in my protective holding tight position, supporting him by the front and back of his belt, slowly navigating this five inch step. Unexpectedly his weak leg buckles, even with a metal brace, and down he goes.

In slow, controlled motion.

Since I have a good hold, he doesn't crash or get hurt, but his legs get all pretzeled together. The right leg is knotted up and stuck like a double-jointed contortionist. Painfully.

Immediately, I figure out what he needs to do to get untangled, but, in typical Michael fashion, he stubbornly resists listening to my directions.

Resists is a tame word.

This goes on for several frantic minutes, the pain becoming excruciating as he ignores my commands, trying to do it his way.

The Right Way.

Finally, out of utter frustration, I take control and yank his now swollen, bruised legs and untangle them. The adrenalin must be pumping because I'm even able to pull his 165 pound body all the way up to a standing position.

Ironically, we are on our way to a physical therapy appointment.

When we arrive, proudly swaggering his freshly black and blue knee, I tell his therapist what just happened. She proceeds to give him a craggy finger lecture about the importance of listening to me.

Like a reprimanded puppy, he listens, but I sense nothing will change.

Mr. Control Freak change? Even after a stroke and a fall? Not going to happen. But really, I know who's in control.

How I Met My Husband

After several months of posting stories exposing my deepest fears, most embarrassing admissions and humorous anecdotes on Facebook, it dawns on me that I've omitted the history of my relationship with Michael pre-stroke.

So, here's the story of how I met my husband.

The world of dating was far more complex than when I divorced husband number one back in 1979. I felt like a fish out of water in this new era of women's equality and casual role definitions.

Me actually call a guy for a date? Impossibly terrifying.

My first year of singlehood clarified that I had no idea what I *really* wanted in a relationship. Based on the many I had dated in the past, I was fairly certain of what I *didn't* want, but not much else.

Having just begun exploring the power of Creative Visualization - the practice of sending out a detailed request to the Universe about what you want to attract - I decided to give it a try. Since I wasn't willing to go out on blind dates and match.com didn't exist yet, I thought, *what the heck!*

Meticulously, I composed a short but detailed list of requests, itemizing them one by one in my journal. Within days, out to dinner with a friend, a cute waiter hit on me. We started dating and, lo and behold, he fit my affirmed requirements precisely. Frighteningly exact!

However, after a few months, I realized he wasn't "The One." Was definitely missing several important qualities I had omitted on my "first draft" affirmation.

Confidence ballooned, I made some alterations to my visualization list, added additional requirements, crossed out what I now realized I didn't want. Closed up my journal and promptly forgot about it.

A few weeks later, the next man arrived, also in an easy and random way. He fit my edited list precisely. Unfortunately, I'd forgotten to include "...lives within thirty miles," and this presented a proximity problem called living 3000 miles away. He wasn't willing to move here and I was permanently rooted to SoCal living.

Next list revision. Next arrival. Repeat several more times.

At the demise of each relationship, I would add more exacting details to my ever-expanding Cosmic Wish List.

In early October 1985, I scribed one last relationship shopping list line item: *"...and, he loves to give massages and doesn't want me to reciprocate."* Figured, if the Universe is providing, I might as well go hog wild with my request! It was up to five pages now, not including the crossed out items and additional specs to existing items.

A week later, Michael walked through my kitchen.

Six months previously, Michael had been an attendee in the spiritual development classes I was teaching. When he and his business partner started renting my garage for their silk screening business, we became casual friends.

Frequently, we'd sit at my kitchen table drinking tea and chatting. He would listen as I described my search for Mr. Right, sharing the latest episodes about the many Mr. Wrongs.

He became good buddies with my nine year old son, taking him to baseball games and other adventures. Michael being so child-like, they adored each other.

On that afternoon in October, my back door opened and in Michael walked, wearing his usual raggedy, paint splattered, corduroy shorts that made a phit-phit sound as they rubbed together.

Smelling like turpentine and sweat, his John Lennon-esque wire-rimmed glasses slipped down his sweaty face. As always, he greeted me with one of his goofy quips, causing me to laugh until my sides ached.

Even though he had previously walked through my kitchen dozens of times, suddenly, almost uncontrollably, my eyes were compelled to look at his muscular, long-distance runner's legs. Weird, I'd never noticed them before.

At that exact moment, I felt a sensation in my heart that could only be described as a "pang." It was at that precise moment I perceived him differently.

Ignoring that intense sensation as best I could, I thought how crazy it was to be attracted to this silly guy several years my junior. *Maybe it's just horniness.* It had been a while, after all.

Spontaneously, without forethought, I asked if he wanted to attend the three day retreat I was conducting the following weekend. Like all my students, he knew about the retreats I held, yet always had lots of excuses to not attend. This time, however, he immediately agreed to go.

Although I cherished my alone drive time, I suggested we drive up together. He said sure.
The two hour drive was replete with frequent bathroom stops to ease his nervously reactive digestive tract. It became a joke, and, as his teacher, I prodded to help him determine why he was reacting so intensely. He resisted admitting how terrified he was, and I just let it go.

The first night of the retreat, Michael hung out downstairs with me after everyone else had gone to bed. He generously offered to give me a neck massage.

Appreciatively, I sat at his feet as his technically untrained, yet incredibly skillful fingers, relaxed every knot. Without warning, I found myself having my first out of body experience! Silently, I went with it, feeling safe in his presence.

After over an hour, he was done. In a daze, I thanked him profusely, also told him what had happened. He had a proud look on his face that he could've somehow facilitated such an experience for his spiritual teacher. He didn't say much, and then went upstairs to bed. I drifted off immediately, having intensely lucid dreams the entire night.

Our drive home together was full of laughter. He effortlessly turned a scary, one working windshield wiper no-visibility, foggy drive down a hairpin curved mountain road into a fun experience.

The Tuesday after the retreat, my phone rang. Shocked, it was Michael asking to take me to lunch! I didn't question this uncharacteristic invitation since, after all, he was my kitchen table buddy and student.

We met at a busy Chinese restaurant near my office. Sitting across from each other, we were suddenly enormously uncomfortable. Our casual friendship became unexpectedly unacknowledged first date awkward.

Engaging in small talk, our eyes wandered uncomfortably toward the tropical fish tank during several prolonged silences.

When there were no more crunchy noodles to munch, we split the bill, grabbed our fortune cookies, and cracked them open as we exited.

Standing by his filthy blue station wagon, laughing at the clichéd messages we both received, we gawkily said our good byes. As I was getting into my car, he slipped a neatly folded envelope with my name on it into my hand.

"What's this?" I asked, vaguely remembering the odd attraction I had felt a few days ago. "Ummm, read it later," his face turned crimson. Before I could reply, he gunned the accelerator and drove off, leaving me clutching the mysterious envelope.

Ignoring his request, I immediately tore it open, read with astonishment his hesitantly expressed, well composed words of love. Timidly covering his bases, it included several "outs" in case those feelings proved unreciprocated.

The biggest shock was his detailed description of being in my kitchen having a sudden intense attraction toward me. You guessed it: *The exact instant I'd been mysteriously attracted to him!*
Hyperventilating, I drove to my office in a daze.

Without mentioning the letter, I left a message on his voice mail inviting him to go trick-or-treating with my son and I the following night.

He arrived right after dinner. The three of us had a great time, all just as wacky as my nine year old.

Afterwards, he waited patiently in my living room while I tried to put my sugar-high child to bed. When he finally settled down, I went to where Michael was sitting, put on a serious face and out popped what would become my infamous line: *"So, what was your intent with the letter?"*

Red-faced stuttering, back-peddling body language, he looked longingly at the front door, ready to bolt. Before he could even try, I put both hands on his shoulders. "Michael, I feel the same way." A sigh heard round the world. A hug. A kiss. Tears. Laughter. Longer hug.

We spent a long time comparing our simultaneous Cupid experience in my kitchen, both dumbfounded at the synchronicity.

A week later, after spending every day together, the "I love you" sentence was revealed. Another week and "The M Word" is stated.

We wrote our own wedding ceremony and got married on December 13th, a little over a month since our first Halloween hug.

Despite warnings from caring friends and family about *taking it slow* (found out that some had even placed bets as to the longevity of our marriage), there was no doubt in our minds that we were destined to be together. It was easy, effortless, and perfect.

So far, this match made in heaven has lasted over three decades.

Honestly, if it wasn't for Cupid's Infinite Wisdom, I never would've perceived this goofy guy who was right under my nose as The One who fit every single one of my visualized requests.

Best of all: He never wanted me to reciprocate massages.

Our union evolved to working as partners, committing to assist others and even the planet. We started and ran an eco-shop/gallery when green wasn't a household word.

Together we helped my students in their transformational growth, him focusing on physical issues, me on the spiritual.

Together we helped re-brand the small village that housed our shop, getting involved in community politics in every way possible.

And now, working on healing from a stroke, sharing this challenging journey together every step of the way.

Never thought this would land on my Life with Michael Resume, but, as always, I do what's put in front of me.

No matter how big.

Things No One Tells You About Strokes

- The affected arm and leg are super sensitive, and hurt like hell even when touched gently or touched with anything cold.
- They will probably become incontinent. Not all the time and always when you least expect it. It may not last long but it could.
- They can't scratch their own back.
- They can't clean or cut their fingernails.
- It can take twenty minutes to get into bed. And out of bed.
- They probably won't remember their name.
- They probably won't remember their spouse's name.
- They probably won't remember your children/grandchildren/sibling/best friend's names.
- They will probably be tired a lot.
- They won't be interested in sex, if they even remember what sex is.
- They might be extremely slow since their eyes are having a hard time focusing. They might be dizzy because of that.
- They may understand everything you say to them but not be able to respond.
- They may not understand anything you say to them.
- They may understand everything you say to them but not be able to follow the simplest of directional commands.
- They may understand everything you say to them but then forget immediately.
- Often they don't care about getting better since the frontal lobe (in charge of motivation) may have been affected.

- Whatever their personality was before might become exaggerated to the extreme or become very child-like.

Popcorn and Empathy

This week we are attending the first segment of a seven week, twice a week, four hour aphasia intensive workshop at Michael's rehab hospital.

We were invited by his speech therapist who saw potential beyond the Neanderthal grunts he still uses (with an occasional word thrown in, often of the four letter persuasion, actually mastering appropriate use of the F-bomb! Woohoo!).

It's informative hearing details about aphasia that I hadn't heard previously and being given edifying tools to cope with this challenge.

When one of the therapists leading the group states that "You are still smart even though you have aphasia!"

This is a question I've been afraid to ask. For some reason, maybe because Michael is so intelligent, it's nice to know. Even though he can't access his smarts just yet. I sigh, relieved and hopeful.

Most of the four hours are spent blowing my nose from non-stop crying. I'm so touched by the stories each participant shares, relating profoundly on this new journey we're all traveling.

Spontaneously, a sixty-ish woman with short gray hair tearfully unleashes her deepest fears since her stroke. This is the first time she's able to express emotions without well-meaning relatives telling her to "just work harder and you'll be fine." Silent reverence fills the room until someone breaks the ice by giving her an empathetic (and gratefully received) hug.

The speech therapist facilitator isn't prepared to do a group therapy session, but she fakes it well. We all connect in some way to what this brave survivor is experiencing.

At the mid-point of the class, family participants are taken to a separate room for a break-out session. We're given a word or phrase with the assignment to get the others to guess it. Like our aphasic partners, we are only allowed a limited number of sounds or gestures to get it across.

Kinda like charades but harder.

The word on my card is "popcorn." The parameters were that I could only say the word "hot" and point to the letter "P" somewhere in the room. Needless to say, it's one of the most difficult things I've ever tried to accomplish.

Tried being the operative word.

Within about three minutes of frantic gesturing and finding the only P in the room to point to, I shrug my shoulders in utter frustration. The therapist throws me a bone by providing a white board where I draw a slapdash picture of popcorn in a theater bag. Even without employing years of art school prowess, the group immediately figures out what I'm trying to say.

Instant empathy toward my aphasic husband. Which is, of course, the point of the exercise.

The other family members have equally humbling experiences with their assigned words.

When we return to the main room to share, I struggle holding back tears. As always, the tears win.

"You know, I'm really good at playing charades, but the limitations made this incredibly difficult. I now totally understand Michael's frustration."

Didn't admit it out loud, but experiencing empathy brings my self-absorbed frustration with Michael down a notch. Or ten. Amazing what walking in someone's shoes can do.

The second day of class is equally powerful.

This time, family members are partnered with a stroke survivor with the simple assignment: Have a conversation! A list of potential chit-chat ideas is provided. Topics such as: *What's your favorite vacation place; where are you from; what's your favorite thing to do.*

Non-coincidentally, I'm paired with the woman who unleashed my bout of tears with her heartfelt confession in class one.

As we sit facing each other on a small couch, she starts expressing even more about what she's going through post stroke. She admits she's unable to sleep and is constantly terrified. Tears flow. Kleenex shared.

"Does your husband experience these things too?" she asks.

"No, he's still in his Happy Place. But," I clear my throat, "I do."

Her eyes widen in shock. Empathy reversal.

I expound, disclosing how scary it was to be his caregiver. I also assure her that all she's (we) feeling is quite "normal" after going through such a life-changing experience.

Not intending to go into my spiritual teacher mode, but it slipped out like a banana squeezed from its peel.
"You know, we're never given more than we can handle." She looks grateful for the reminder. Especially when I add my personal addendum: "But that sure doesn't make it any easier, right?" We share a knowing smile.

And an empathetic hug.

My attention veers to Michael working with his partner across the room. They're laughing uncontrollably as he tries to get her to figure out the answer to something asked from their suggested topic sheet.

I mosey over to check out the situation.

The question they're concentrating on is "What sport do you like to do?" His partner had written down an extensive list of sports, each with a line crossing out the ones she guessed incorrectly.

I jump into the guessing game since, if anyone knows what sports Michael likes to do it would be me. Rapid fire, I throw out suggestions: "Bowling?" I ask confidently. No. "Tennis?" No. "Baseball?" NO!

He's now rolling his eyes and shaking his head at my pathetic attempts at figuring out what should be obvious after double digit years together.

"Michael, what about running?" He'd been a runner in high school with a natural penchant for it, but hasn't run in years. "Well, nooooo....!" he says, getting ever more annoyed.

"What about long distance running?" Sometimes Michael is annoyingly persnickety about details, even post stroke.

"Nooooo...." but there's hope in his voice that maybe I'm heading in the right direction.
"Sprinting?" More eye-rolling but he gestures that I'm getting warmer.

About to give up, it hits me. "Is it track?"

"YES!!!!"

Duh.

Apologizing to his partner about how picky this man is, we both breathe a sigh of empathetic relief.

Steppin' Out

We're invited to a Big Five-0 birthday party taking place the Saturday before Mother's Day.

I'm looking forward to it for lots of reasons. Not the least of which is seeing people I haven't seen in a long time; good food; doing something other than watching TV, running errands, cleaning the house and being Michael's full time caregiver.

Not that there's anything wrong with all that. Just a bit of cabin fever.

As we get dressed I'm noticing that Michael isn't looking real enthused about going. "What's going on Michael?" I ask.

He shakes his head pathetically. Scrunching up his nose, he makes his *something is wrong* grunt.

"Are you okay?" I ask.

"Well, yes. No. I don't know," he replies.

I start my 20 question routine. "Are you feeling okay?" "Yes." "Are you tired?" "No." "Is it something about the party?" "Yes!" Bullseye. "Do you not want to go?" "Yes!" "Oh, okay, why?"

Asking *why* questions is pretty futile, but out it pops, force of habit.

He frowns and struggles to find words. No words come. More struggle.

Suddenly, I hear what sounds like a word. "Shaaarah"

"What did you say Michael?"

"Sharalht" even more garbled.

"Um, I can't quite understand what you are saying," but I persist. For about ten minutes. Like a broken record.

Suddenly he says it clearly: "Char!"

"Oh wow, are you talking about Charlotte?"

Charlotte is our 8 year old granddaughter.

"Yes!" He explodes with exhilaration that I'm finally able to understand something as simple as our granddaughter's name.

I start putting two and two together. "Michael, we are going to see Charlotte and Zoe (our other granddaughter) tomorrow on Mother's day."

He shakes his head violently and says "NO!"

Another ten minutes of bantering back and forth.

Again, I figure out what's going on. "Michael, do you think it's Mother's Day today?"

"YESH!" Oh geez.

"No, Mother's Day is tomorrow! And we will see the girls then!"

He isn't quite buying it. "Really," I assure him, taking out my cell phone calendar, showing it as proof.

"Is that why you don't want to go to the party today?"

At this point it's way too late to get there. Maybe I didn't really want to go either.

"Yes," he replies gloomily.

The next day at my son's house I tell Charlotte what her G-Pa said. "You mean he didn't even say Zoe's name?"

"Nope, just yours!" Her face glows.

She outshined her twin sister and that's always the best thing in her life, ever.

To Change the World

Sitting at Michael's speech therapy group this week, the Thursday after New Year's, I realize that these rehab people have become family. Family that gets what you're going through and knows exactly what to say. Or not say. Family that never judges, criticizes or has expectations.

They just know.

The meeting is casual this week. The therapist usually brings some kind of speech activity or exercise, but she has no agenda, just winging it, allowing it to flow organically.

After asking how everyone's New Year's Eve was, she poses a group question: *What's your wish to have happen in the new year?*

The post-holiday group is small, just four participants and myself. One of the loyal attendees is a young man, maybe thirty at the most, but it's hard to tell. He's nicely dressed, well- groomed with a perfectly trimmed, ebony brown beard.

Don't know details about the whys of his physical condition, but he's completely wheel chair bound, not able use his hands or do much of anything himself. His mother is his full time caregiver, and I've seen her lovingly feeding him in the cafeteria.

When he first began attending the group, it seemed he was unable to speak, but each week he would talk a little bit more when prodded. His words are difficult to understand, like a record playing on the wrong speed, unintelligible unless you really slow your listening down. However, he knows precisely what he wants to say and eventually gets it out.

This week showed that it's worth the wait.

Whenever he says anything, his words end with a sing-songy

up-tone, a toothy grin and always punctuated with a child-like giggle finale. His laugh is so engaging that it's impossible to not laugh with him. Even though he doesn't say anything funny.

So, when the therapist directs her question at him, asking what his new year wish is, it takes a minute, but his words bring tears to my eyes.

Slowly and clearly he says: *"To change the world."*

The silence in the room is palpable. If Michael could speak, I know he would have cracked one of his infamous pre-stroke jokes to break the seriousness. But today, he sits with the rest of us, mesmerized in stunned silence by what this man expresses with such insightful eloquence.

Finally, I break the silence.

Looking across the room at him, trying hard to hold back the flood of tears trying to escape, I say "Wow, what an awesome thing to wish for!"

Especially since everyone else's wish list consists of more mundane desires like eating healthy, planting a garden, and Michael's request to see his almost nine year old granddaughters more often.

Seeing gratitude in his eyes for acknowledging his wish, my thoughts swirl with what I *really* want to say. Not sure of its appropriateness, I bite my tongue to stop myself from saying "Well, if there's anyone that's going to be able to change the world, it's you!"

Clearly, this young man, even with labored, 45 rpm words and a body without volitional control, makes quite an impact wherever he goes.

Which starts me thinking about the Universe. The wacky yet always Perfect way it gets us where we're supposed to be, to get the lessons we need to get or give to others.

Early on when I began my spiritual teaching, I would always think that somehow, someday, the information I'd been "gifted" with, was going to have a bigger impact. Even though I chose to keep the classes small, I sensed that, eventually, something would shift and I'd be reaching lots more people.

However, envisioning standing at a podium surrounded by thousands of seekers, or having my own television show never felt right. Clearly, the power of the teachings I present is in the intimacy of the group, students being accountable and present, rather than just an anonymous member of a crowd.

Never in a zillion years did I think my messages would be delivered through something called *social media*. And certainly never thought it would be because my husband had a debilitating stroke.

But here I am, writing words from my heart that so many are telling me are meaningful and touching their lives.

Go figure.

So, my social media family, here's to a new year bursting with opportunities for all of us to change the world. We all can, and we all do in our own Perfect ways.

Even if we are doing it using very slow words and don't even realize it.

Or are just posting random thoughts on Facebook.

Numbers Count

Although his vocabulary has increased a bit since his stroke six months ago, Michael's biggest struggles is retrieving words.

Struggles is the understatement of the century.

He knows exactly what he wants to say, but it still comes out in a strange language that only he understands. It still combines Neanderthal and grunts, with some ancient African dialect minus the clicking sounds thrown in.

But lately, this former math genius, has started using numbers to try to communicate.

To him it makes perfect sense. Like the number two means Tuesday. Sometimes. Sometimes it means us. Sometimes it means the second month.

Interpreting this new code is my challenge.

Depending on what he's trying to say, numbers take on different meanings. And they change like the weather.

Like the other day.

He suddenly starts rattling off numbers frantically. He keeps repeating "six," more and more emphatically.

After about thirty minutes of trying to guess what he's alluding to, I ask him to try writing it. He puts pen to paper and writes a line of horizontal numbers, one through six. He then writes another line of numbers intersecting vertically with that one and starts pointing to the center repeatedly. "Six, six, SIX!" Again and again.

Suddenly I have a thought. "Does this have something to do with a date?"

I remember what we had gone through in March when he had urgently tried to communicate that it was his long-deceased father's birthday.

"YES!" he answers, happy that his wife is finally starting to get what's so obvious to him.

I produce a wall calendar and he immediately turns to the last month. "December?" I ask. "Yes!"

Okay, so, something to do with Christmas? "No!" How about our son's birthday? "No!" The only other December event is our anniversary. "So, is it our anniversary?" His answer is a yes with a hesitant lilt in his voice.

"Michael, you know it's not December, right?" He gives me one of his "duh" looks and continues jabbing-pointing to the six in the middle of the two lines of numbers.

Another ten minutes going back and forth, more sixes, more guesses, more frustration, more eye rolling toward a wife that just doesn't have a clue!

Then, miraculously, the heavens part: I figure it out.

"Michael, are you trying to say that it's our six month anniversary?"

"YES!!"

OMG. I laugh until I cry. It's so touching, that, of all things to still have a synapse for, this is one.

Back in the pre-stroke day, he would occasionally catch me off guard to spontaneously inform that we'd been married a certain amount of days, right down to the hour.

I hug and thank him. I'm reminded, once again, that he's all in there just trying to get out.

Hurry please.

More Numbers

Today we have another episode of numbering, this one even more cryptic.

His fabulous seven week speech therapy intensive is in its last week. The patients were given an ongoing project to take themed photographs and then compose captions for them. The goal was to create an exhibit at the rehab hospital to celebrate National Aphasia Month.

Despite a lot of resistance to do the assignment, Michael took some amazing pictures. However, the creative captions he came up with really gave them personality. Michael's humor came through, of course, with me as translator.

He calls me over to his side in the middle of the afternoon, once more trying to communicate something. Again with numbers.

"Four!" he says. Based on what he often means, I ask if four means Friday. "Yes!"

A few more questions and then "Do, you want to know what we're doing on Friday?" "Yes!" I remind him about the photography exhibit and he nods his head excitedly.

In a rather circuitous way, he expresses that he wants to invite someone to the showing. "Who do you want to invite, Michael?"

Out pops the word "EVERYONE!" without hesitation.

Wow. I love when random words emerge spontaneously like that.

"Anyone in particular?" I press.

He goes into number code mode again.

"One, two, three, four, five!" he keeps insisting. He points to his fingers and when he gets to five he emphasizes that number. Using what worked last time, I ask if he's talking about a particular date.

"No!" A month? "No!"

"Michael, this number stuff is really frustrating! Can you try to write a word or draw a picture instead?"

One thing I've gathered from his speech class is to not just aim to for words, but try whatever tactics will work. It's all about communication, no matter what form it takes. Quite a relief.

He insists on continuing with numbers. When he says "two" he starts pointing to himself. I say, "Michael?" and he says yes. I'm on to something.

"Okay, so two is Michael."

"YES!" Bingo.

"So, you want to invite yourself?" He laughs and says no.

He then starts pointing at his index finger and says *one* repeatedly. Okay, so if two is Michael, who is one?

"Is one someone you want to invite to your exhibit?"
"Yes!" We go back and forth, me guessing various people, friends, family members. I name every person I can think of to no avail. He keeps pointing east, looking off in the distance.

This goes on for fifteen frustrating minutes. We both want to give up but we're in too deep.

"Okay Michael, I can't do this anymore. Please either draw a picture or try to write their name!" I gave him a piece of paper and a pen. Guess what? He writes down 1,2,3,4,5.

What the F!

He then circles the number two and writes the word "sis" next to it. I had already asked if he wants to invite his sisters and he said yes, but clearly there was more to what he's trying to say.

He then circles the number one and writes the word DAD next to it.

Suddenly the lightbulb flickers on. *I coulda had a V-8.*

"Michael, are you talking about your brother Jim?" It's as if I solved the mysteries of the universe!

"YES!!!"

Wow, amazing. His brother was the first child in the family, thus the number one. Michael arrived next and then three more siblings, all girls. Thus the 1,2,3,4,5 emphasis.

Unfortunately his brother lives out of state, but I know he would be at the exhibit if he were in town.

Ever notice how problems always look easy once they're solved?

Take Me Out!

A bunch of people from Michael's speech therapy group bought tickets to a Dodger game and we all meet there. Michael is so excited he can hardly stand it, being the baseball fan(atic) that he is.

Baseball is definitely not my thing, to put it mildly. I think it's the one interest that Michael and I don't have in common, but I tolerate going to games once a year (under duress) as long as I can either bring a book to read or play games on my cell phone.

It drives him crazy, but it's better than sleeping through it, right?

My biggest concern about going to Dodger Stadium is the bathroom situation. Bowing to his insistence, we've been using the men's rooms. I've become fairly immune to accompanying him as long as they're small enough to check to make sure the urinals aren't being used.

Based on the size of the venue, I figure this will be a huge issue. Hoping for a caregiver bathroom, I don't see any on their website.

A few days before the game, I voice my concern to the speech therapy group. One of the "able bodied" men volunteers to accompany Michael to the bathroom. Phew. Problem solved, so I don't think any more about it.

Until we get to the game.

Apparently, when you get tickets for someone in a wheelchair, they put you in a balcony-like area where you don't have to navigate the treacherous steep stairs. Somehow the seats are confused, and the usher tells us we'll have to walk down a long flight of stairs to get to our assigned spots. I look at her and look at Michael sitting in his wheelchair and explain how that just won't work.

After several minutes of confusion (Usher: "Sorry, all the wheelchair seating is filled."), she offers to have me sit in a regular seat and leave Michael somewhere else.

Not acceptable.

It takes every ounce of strength (and looking at Michael's disappointed face) to not storm out in frustration, so when a stranger offers up their disabled designated spot to us, I gratefully accept.

After calming down and settling in, I look around for the others in our group. We all have tickets together, but from where we   are now seated, I can't find any of them in a sea of Dodger blue regalia.

Especially the generous man who volunteered bathroom escort duty.

Feeling somewhat panicked at the thought of wheeling Michael into this very public men's room, I spend the entire game scanning every row looking for this man. To no avail.

During the seventh inning stretch, I look over at Michael (at full volume singing his Neanderthal rendition of Take Me Out to the Ballgame) and state firmly: "Michael, *you will just have to go to the bathroom yourself and I know you can   do it and I trust you will be just fine."* (Who am I *really* trying to convince?)

He looks at me and says *yes*, but I notice he stops drinking the bottled water we brought. Even though it's mid-summer, 80 degrees and he's ravenously consumed two veggie dogs.

At last, the ninth boring inning is done (okay, all baseball games are boring to me, but this one is particularly slow with two runs in the first inning and nothing else for the rest of the game. Yawn!).

Just to be polite, I ask Michael if he has to go to the bathroom, reminding him that he's going solo. He says no (maybe all liquid has been sweated out in this heat?) and, although we have a 40 minute drive home, I breathe a sigh of relief.

We wait until the crowds quell and start the long roll back to our car (which, annoyingly, they didn't have a disabled space available for, even though we got there forty minutes early). Wheeling past several men's rooms, suddenly Michael motions to one, indicating that yes, he *does* have to go.

Reminding him again that I'm not going in with him, I ask if he's okay with that. He nods a decidedly clear and confident *yes*.

Nervously, I wheel his chair to the entrance, instructing that if he desperately needs me, just scream.

Part of me knows he will be fine (*what's the worst that could happen, after all?*), and another part is scared as hell. But, as he rolls in without me, he seems self-assured and completely unconcerned, a totally new independent attitude from him.

I wait by the door trying to trust.

I've written previously that Michael is very, very slow at toileting, so a fifteen minute wait is not unusual. However, since I'm not with him, it seems interminable.

Each minute that inches by I debate going in to bravely rescue him. Each time I'm about to, more men go in and thwart my plan.

Seeing two uniformed cops walking toward me I wonder:

Can I be arrested for loitering outside the men's room?

Simultaneously, I entertain the idea that I could get their help to check on (and perhaps save) Michael. I imagine his surprise at having two police officers knocking at his stall! Might speed things up permanently (or scare the you-know-what out of him!)!

As they come close enough to engage for help (or arrest me for lurking outside a men's room), out rolls Michael, beaming proud as a peacock at his latest accomplishment.

"Michael, I'm so proud of you! You did it! How did it go? Did everything work out okay?" My list of questions that I knew can't be answered pour out anyway.

Noticing he has a funny look on his face motivates even more questions. "You *did* go to the bathroom, right?" He nods his head. "Why that look?" He shrugs his good shoulder, not able (or willing) to reply.

I just know *something* happened.

Sometimes his underwear is a challenge to pull up. "Did you just leave your underpants in the bathroom?" That's a solution   he would think to do, clever man that he is.

"No!" he insists.

"Were you able to flush?" That's also difficult when trying to balance, pull up shorts and get back on a wheelchair using one   leg and one hand.

"No," he admits.

"It's okay, I don't care. You succeeded at this and I'm so excited!" His funny look doesn't subside. .

Thoughts of being able to go places we haven't gone simply because of awkward bathroom situations overwhelm me. Selfishly, I feel a surge of freedom at not having to perform a task that's not my most favorite thing to do.

To say the least.

Most importantly, I'm thrilled that Michael has taken one more step toward post stroke liberation.

I may never know what actually happened in the men's room at Dodger Stadium, but I do know that not locating the man who volunteered to take Michael in was the best thing about the entire evening.   I will thank him profusely at our next therapy session.

After listening politely to how great the game was.

Yawn.

Get In!

Here's a parables I recite to my students ad nauseam:

There's a man climbing to safety on the roof of his house as flood waters rise. He's praying frantically to God, beseeching to rescue him. As the water gets higher, a row boat arrives with the rower shouting "Get in!"

Instead of taking him up on his offer and paddling to safety, he explains, "I'm praying to God to rescue me, so thanks but no thanks."

A while later, a helicopter circles above him, drops a rope ladder down and the pilot shouts "Climb up! You're going to drown!" Refusing, once more explaining that he's waiting for God to rescue him.

Needless to say, the flood engulfs his house and the man drowns.

When he arrives at the pearly gates and meets God face-to-face, he says, angrily, "God, I prayed and prayed that you would rescue me. Why didn't you answer my prayers?" God replies with a sheesh (if God can sheesh) "My son, I sent you a row boat and a helicopter, why didn't you get in?"

The point of the story is that sometimes we are being handed a perfect and quite miraculous solution to a problem, but, because we think it should look a different way, we don't see what's arriving to save us.

Like the situation I'm in right now.

The last eight months since Michael's debilitating stroke have been trying on every level. I closed our twenty-one year shop, stopped teaching after thirty-five years and became his full time caregiver. It's been beyond a stretch financially to do this, but my priority is being there for him, helping 100% in his recovery.

The Universe (or God) always shows me in obvious ways what I'm supposed to do (if I'm open to seeing the blatant or sometimes subtle signs), so I keep asking: *What's next for us?*

Freelance writing gigs started landing in my lap in interesting ways, and I've fallen *madly* in love with doing that. It's feeding my soul and I know I've found at least part of my third career.

But the helicopter of all amazing miracles had me quite inadvertently arrive in a Desert Hot Springs healing center.

Condensed version: Almost two years ago, by a fluke, I was hired to write an article for a website about a revolutionary drug rehab treatment. I did, and it helped the business go berserk with new customers.

I never heard from her again until about a month ago when she emailed to ask if I knew what to do about someone plagiarizing my article on their website! Besides being flattered that someone would do that, I had no idea what to advise.

Meanwhile, I told her about Michael's stroke and she excitedly told me about a healing place using hyperbaric oxygen that I simply must take him to. I explained our financial situation and she assured me that "something could be worked out with the owner cause he sure needs someone to do some writing for him."

I almost shined it, but a wiser part of me said, what the heck, it couldn't hurt to chat. I rarely ignore such serendipitous events.

The first conversation with the owner was futile. Not at all how I would imagine a healing resort owner to be: He was direct, a little intimidating and quite gruff. Attentive but distracted, he didn't respond when I told him who had referred me and what I had accomplished for her business with my article. He said he would get back to me, and I thought for sure I'd never hear from him again.

Meanwhile, I contacted the person I wrote the article for and told her it didn't look like he was interested in doing a trade. She said, "don't worry... it will work out. No doubt."

Her words were filled with such confidence that I decided to trust completely. No sooner than I did, the owner called me back. After a few conversations, he said he'd be willing to do a trade for writing.

I was blown away by his generosity (hyperbaric treatments are not cheap!), packed our bags and drove off to Desert Hot Springs. In July. Never so hot in my life.

The minute we arrived, this magical yet very grounded place felt like home. I tried to fight the feeling since I'm not a desert girl at all, but it was like a bungee cord: Every time I would think about not being here, I felt a tug insisting to get my butt back there!

Thus, we are now here for the third time, and my list of writing assignments grows with each twenty hours of hyperbaric oxygen Michael inhales

Even with my little skeptical mind yapping away, it's clear that I'm supposed to be part of this place in some way. Before I get the nerve up to even suggest it to the owner, he approaches me with his ideas of how it could work.

We've been talking daily as my role in everything he's doing keeps expanding. Seems like a perfect fit, especially since about 25 years ago I stated to the Universe that I wanted a spiritual retreat healing center!

Who knew it would manifest like this, and take 25 years to get here!

And yet, I hesitate.

Why, you might ask? Well, from what I can tell, it could only be one of two things: *Fear rearing its unshaven face.* Or some notion I have that it's not supposed to be this easy.

Silly me.

Sure, it would mean changing everything in my life. Selling my house. Moving to the desert. Starting anew. But it feels so right, so effortless, so smooth.

Like everything that's ever happened in my life has been preparing me to be right here.

The litmus test was asking Michael what we should do.

As I described previously, he's not one who takes to making changes real easily. To say the least. However, when I

ask, *Michael, do you think we should just sell our house and move here and be part of this,* he looks at me with absolute clarity and said "YES!" with a slight duh at the end of his short response.
Is this my helicopter moment?

As we get ready to leave for home in a few minutes, Michael is in tears but I assure him we will be back.

Is this just desert intoxication?

One Small Step

Michael's weak right side causes a great deal of struggle when trying to walk.

Admittedly, I'm more focused on wanting speech to come back (tired of monologues with my Neanderthal man) so haven't mentioned much about his journey toward walking.

In the rehab hospital they explain that leg movement is often the first to return. It's a primitive survival thing, they say, our anciently wired bodies needing to run from danger more than pick their dirty loin cloths off the cave floor or have profound discussions with saber tooth tigers.

Or their mates.

Their assessment is accurate. Michael started moving his leg months ago, but isn't able to get very far without a lot of wifely assistance and a four-pronged cane. Even then, it's snail's pace, and a short walk from the bedroom to the bathroom in our tiny house gets him winded.

Winded isn't the right word. More like exhausted. Panting. Done. Needs a nap.

Our legs do so much more than walk. Think about it. How do you get off a chair? Get into a bath? Get into or out of bed? They are pretty useful appendages to have, and when they don't work it affects just about everything.

Especially our sense of independence.

The last time our eight year old granddaughter came to visit she looked at Michael and said with a very sad face "I feel so sorry for G-Pa." I asked her why and she explained that "He can't go where he wants to go."

Profoundly caring child.

At our latest visit to the Desert Hot Springs healing center, I tell Michael it's time to go for his hyperbaric oxygen treatment. Imagine my surprise when he gets out of bed and is standing their waiting for me... by himself!

I guess surprise isn't the right word. Jumping up and down thrilled would be a more accurate description.

Sharing the news with the resort director, I can hardly contain my excitement. He isn't at all surprised, smiles and says, "Of course! More to come!"

After his treatment, Michael does another miraculous feat: He walks by himself from the bed to the bathroom! Once there, he actually pulls down his shorts and pulls them back up by himself (yes, I've been doing all that for eight months...)! Immediate sighs of relief at the thought of not having to take him into public toilets anymore . Not sure who's happier with this accomplishment!

Can't wait to see what he has next in his bag of reconnecting synapse tricks!

P.S. His pant-pulling ability comes and goes. I think he just likes me to do it for him. Typical male, right?

A Present of Presence

Tonight when we get back to our room after Michael's hyperbaric oxygen treatment, he tries to verbalize something. His garbled speech is still tough to decipher. To say the least. Which he does.

Combining charades, knowing him well, and being pretty psychically attune, I can usually figure out what he's trying to say. Eventually.

But today's a stumper.

"Where?" he asks. Sometimes he uses words that aren't exactly what he means. Especially the who, what, where, when and how words.

"Where? Michael, do you want to know where are we?" I ask?

"Yes."

"We are in Desert Hot Springs at the medical resort."

"NO! Where?" he insists.

"Our room? The living room?" I try a few obvious answers but nothing works.

"Where are you?" He points to me as he gets out a three word sentence, an incredible feat!

"Um, I'm here, with you, in Desert Hot Springs, at the healing resort, in the living room!"

Trying to cover all possible places where I could possibly be.

Nope, not what he wants to hear, but I'm thrilled he strung three words together.

He keeps pointing at me, repeating the same question with more frustration.

"Michael, if you are asking whether I'm present with you 100% I am. Cell phone is away. Computer is closed. No distractions for once. Is that what you mean?"

"No!"

"I don't know Michael, I have no idea what you're asking about, but we need to eat dinner. Maybe it will come to you later."

He looks dejected as he always does when dense wife can't figure out what's so obvious to him.

After dinner the conversation continues. To no avail. I let it drop and help him with his exercises.

After doing more writing and marketing for the resort, I crawl into bed about 12:30. Michael is wide awake watching some old black and white gangster movie.

Reluctantly he turns it off.

As we cuddle, he brings up the enigmatic question again. This time he adds the word Saturday.

"Yes, it's Saturday, but actually it's Sunday now."

"YES!" he's thrilled I'm finally on the right track.

"Okay, so it's Sunday, August second. Is that significant in some way?" I'm remembering his desperation to have me remember his Dad's birthday.

I take a leap.

"Is it something to do with your Dad?" I ask, since that relationship is always number one in importance to him.

"YES!!" he says with relief.

"Oh my God," I get it. A vague memory of his Dad dying in early August flitters into my mind. "Was this the day your dad died?"

"YES!!!!!!"

Geez. Louise. I take out my phone and enter it in my calendar. Click on "repeat forever" so I will always remember.

"That was a long time ago, Michael. How many years? I think at least 25."

"NO," he says with utmost confidence. He's always right about these things.

I do the math. It's 28 years ago that his dad passed.

Suddenly, I have the strongest feeling that his dad is visiting us. That happens once-in-a-while to me since I'm open and sensitive to such "visitations." The minute I recognize and acknowledge his Dad's presence my entire left side gets tingly-numb.

"Michael, was your dad's stroke on his left side?"

"Yes."

"Wow, I'm so feeling him here right now."

Often, when spirits are attempting to communicate, they give physical sensations to identify themselves and to add verification that they are 'real.' I still have my skeptical moments, but I can't deny what my body is experiencing.

A thirty minute "conversation" ensues. We're both in tears as his dad relays so many memories and random thoughts. I share them all with his aphasic son.

"Michael, did your dad have a great sense of humor like you?" I had only known Al for two years when Michael and I got married. And, it was after he already had his stroke, so he was pretty quiet and serious at that point.

"Yes!!" Michael confirms, nodding his head excitedly and chuckling with memories he can't verbalize.

It still amazes me when I "get" something that ends up being accurate. Only been doing this for four decades!

Suddenly, I feel Michael's Mom's presence join in. I welcome her. She's pretty "quiet" but I feel her strongly.

They both want us to know that we are doing the right thing having hyperbaric treatments. I thank them for the confirmation. Always good to get approval from The Other Side.

I ask for their help in any way they can. Apparently, they are happy to do so, and have been doing some non-physical realm orchestrating already.

More conversation. More memories. More interesting tidbits.

At 1:30 I'm finally able to convince them that us physical humans need some sleep. Reluctantly they make their exit, but it's good to know we aren't "alone" in this.

The Morales team is helping.

P.S. Found out today that after seven months of waiting, Michael is going to be assessed to see if he's a good candidate for stem cell research! Very excited for this possibility! Driving to Arizona in a couple of weeks to be tested... yippee!

Spaghetti Brain

When Michael was still in the rehab hospital fresh after his stroke, he looked at me in frustration when he couldn't access words to express needing to go to the bathroom. Trying to explain what was going on in his brain, I came up with using *spaghetti brain* as a not-very-medically-accurate analogy.

"Well, it's kinda like the synapses in your brain are all tangled up like a plate of spaghetti ... they're confused and jumbled and disconnected." I think he understood but it was hard to tell since, well, his noodle was all spaghettied. At least the analogy made sense to me.

Tonight I experience another indication as to how far he still needs to go.

We're staying in one of the residential rooms at the healing resort as Michael undergoes more intensive hyperbaric oxygen therapy. It has a fully equipped kitchen so I'm cooking all our meals. So much for a vacation, right?

Tonight's main course is spaghetti with sautéed tofu and vegies. After serving him, Michael sits there like a statue, staring hard at his plate piled high with food. He looks confused and starts gesturing, trying frantically to express something about what's in front of him.

I do my usual: Ask lots of questions until I can eventually figure out what he's trying to say. Usually. Not always.

"Is it too much food?" I ask, noticing that he has at least twice as much as what I put on my plate.

"No!" he answers before I can explain why I gave him so much more that I gave myself.

"Is there not enough sauce?" There's never enough sauce for him.

"No!"

"Are you not hungry?"

"NO!"

Volcanic frustration mounts as Ms. Oblivious can't figure out what he's trying to ask.

Finally, he picks up his fork, sticks it in the pile of noodles and they all fall off. The failsafe charades technique gets across that he doesn't know how to eat it.

Holy shit.

My husband, who, I would safely say, has eaten spaghetti hundreds of times in his life, has forgotten the twirling-on-the-fork slurping-up-the-rest technique!

Shocked, never in a million years would I have guessed that was what he's trying to say.

Making light of it, I perform a funny, overly dramatized, step-by-step demonstration as to how one eats spaghetti. The synapse re-fires as he catches on quickly. Twirling each forkful so that only a few noodles bypass his mouth and need slurping: Success.

He expresses gratitude for the lesson and for how yummy my dinner creation is. He devours every last strand.
Since I have half the amount of food, I finish way before him. I excuse myself from the table, go into the bathroom, sit on the toilet and cry.

Just when I think spaghetti brain is getting a bit untangled, a reminder of how far he still needs to go.

According to the doctor here, it usually takes twenty or more hyperbaric treatments before there's any noticeable improvement. "We're flooding the brain and blood cells with pressurized oxygen which helps regenerate injured tissues, especially in traumatic brain injuries like strokes. I don't even start assessing a patient until the twentieth session," he explains.

The theory behind hyperbaric treatment is simple: Since the brain was deprived of oxygen in a stroke, give it oxygen to heal it. Like when you're dehydrated, you drink water. Or starving, you eat food.

Simple logic. Makes sense.

When the doctor finds out we only committed to stay a week, he's adamant about telling me that. Repeats himself several times in various ways along with the confident assurance that Michael should make lots of improvement since his stroke was relatively recent.

Holding back tears, I hear him loud and clear.

After he leaves I cry in Michael's arms. "What should we do?" I ask. Michael answers with one of the few sentences he has mastered: "I don't know."
I take that as a yes, gotta do it. No matter what.

Needless to say, I quickly make arrangements to stay another week.

Remembering how to eat spaghetti? His slurping synapse joins together. Making sure his brain is flooded with oxygen? One more step for mankind.

One of These Days?

Although I don't give credence to this expression, for lack of a better way to express it, I'm going to use it: *Yesterday was "one of those days."*

Starts out fine – we eat breakfast, take Michael down for his hyperbaric oxygen treatment, post the blog I wrote last night, work on the website I'm writing and designing for the healing resort, eat lunch, try to work on the website again but it won't cooperate, more oxygen treatment, dinner, several games of Connect Four (Michael beats me consistently!), set husband in front of the TV and start blogging.

But something feels off. Especially since I unreasonably fly off the handle at Michael for being so slow getting out of his chair. Really, Royce, come on.

Here's a list of some potential reasons:
- I'm exhausted and burned out
- Although I tried really hard not to, admittedly I have some pretty big expectations for his six days of treatment here. I see real progress (lots of new words and a few two word sentences pop out consistently, a greater ability to stand and he even has some feeling in his shoulder!) but he still isn't able to speak in whole sentences like I hoped for. The doctor says not to expect any significant changes until the 20th treatment and we are up to eleven so far. But who's counting?
- I'm exhausted.
- Did I mention I might be burned out?

Although there is a smattering of truth in each of these reasons, none feels completely accurate.

Deciding to do what I always do when I'm not sure what the heck is going on in me, I talk to Michael until I can figure it out. Even back when he was able to speak, he's my best sounding board. All I need really.

"Michael, I'm sorry I was so irritated with you earlier, but I'm feeling weird and I don't know why."

Response: Attentive but blank stare.

"I think I'm just tired and irritated, but you and I know that just means something deeper is going on."

Head nods and slight knowing smile.

"Okay, so what I think's going on is I don't feel deserving of being here. Even though I'm doing a ton of work for them, I feel as though it's never enough. Just my usual belief about myself and my life....I can never do enough; I'm never enough."

He looks at me in amazement, knowing how much time and effort I've been putting into their press releases, websites and promo literature. If he could talk, here's what he'd be saying right now: *Geez Royce, get over it!*

Besides a few freelance writing gigs here and there, it's been a long time since I've actually done work for someone other than myself.

It's interesting to observe how quickly I take ownership. Within two days of working here, I already have the same sense of responsibility I feel toward anything I think is important for the planet: *There's so much valuable, life-*

changing treatments going on here, I just have to get the word out about this place! It's so important that it succeeds!

Sounds familiar, right?

A further sign shows up as a text from a dear, very tuned in friend: *Have you thought that maybe you're supposed to be part of this place in a bigger way, maybe offer your inner development classes and retreats here, do your spiritual work as a needed adjunct to the physical work?*

She reminded me of what I've envisioned since I started teaching 35 years ago: *Having a retreat center.*

So, maybe this whole experience has fallen into my lap because there's something much Bigger about it than my little brain can conceive of.

One of the concepts I continuously teach, and try to remember, is (pardon the cliché) *everything happens for a reason.* It can take years or lifetimes to understand all the whys, but everything is part of the Bigger Picture of our life.

So, maybe everything that happened in the last seven months – Michael's stroke, closing our shop and my office -- has been leading me right here. In the middle of the desert. In an incredible healing place. Surrounded by amazing, dedicated people who have the same intention: To help others.

At this moment in time, I'm not sure, but I'm certainly open to the possibility that there's truth in that. And I'm open to see what the Universe puts in front of me next.

It's a Sign!

Sometimes I believe in signs. More so than I probably should. Especially when they are so bizarre that I just have to stop and take notice.

Or get a cup to remove them.

The day we are scheduled to head to the healing resort for hyperbaric treatments I got up early. As I eat breakfast in our living room and answer emails, I hear a strange buzzing and flapping sound, like a combination bird/bee.

It doesn't take long to find where it's coming from.

Perched on the inside of my window is a four inch, transparent-winged dragonfly. Just sitting there. Minding her own business. If dragonflies have business. And yes, in my mind, it's a girl.

What added to the weird factor was there's no possible way she could've gotten into my house. You think I would've noticed something the size of a small bird flying in. Rematerializing through a screen?

For quite a while I've felt a special kinship with these whirling, allusive creatures, especially when I read how they live their lives. Basically, they wallow around in muddy places and then, when they determine they're ready, they spread their wings and rise from the muck in full glory.

Which is pretty much how I've been feeling these last seven months since Michael's stroke. The wallowing in the mud part.
Being nose-to-nose with Ms. Dragonfly, I allow myself a moment of hopefulness: Maybe she is the bearer of good news, assuring that our week of treatments will be helping us out of the muck of stroke-ness.

It's time to wake up Michael. Immediately, I excitedly tell him about the dragonfly. Luckily I'd taken a picture because, of course, he doesn't believe me. Especially when I go back to the window where she was hanging out and she's gone. Vanished. Into thin air.

Looking everywhere, I figure she returned back to the ether where she had come from because I can find neither hide nor wing of her.

Or, that since I got the message, she didn't need to be there anymore. Wish I coulda at least waved goodbye.

After breakfast, I finish loading up the car. I go back to load Michael. As the cane and I supported him on his slow walk through the living room, the dragonfly is there again in the exact same location.

"Look Michael, see, there she is! I wasn't fantasizing her!" He looks at Ms. D-fly in amazement. "She's back!" I squeal like I'd seen the queen.

After depositing him in the car, I go back in to check on her and determine what to do. Can't leave her in the house for a week. I fetch a cup and gently coax her in, cooing, *come on Ms. Dragonfly*, thanking her for the message she brought.

Gingerly, I take her over to the car and explain to Michael that we need to say an affirmation and set her free.

I'm not sure what his silent prayer is, but mine is enough for both of us: *Healing.* I take my hand off the cup and release her. Off she flies into the clear blue sky, having accomplished her dispatch job.

On our only potty stop halfway to the desert, further winged messages of confirmation arrive. Getting out of the car at the gas station, I feel tugged to look up. About twenty feet away, circling, weaving and bobbing close above us is a red-tailed hawk. Showing just for us, it dances at least five minutes, skillfully performing its aerial ballet to our utter amazement.

Once done toileting, we make our way back to the car, only to be surprised by the most remarkable insect. Iridescent green wings attached to a plump black body flies right at us.

"Okay, Michael, this is so amazing. I guess I really can't ignore all these signs that this week is going to be incredible."

He looks at me with That Look I'd often get when being a bit too "out there" for his more logical-based reality. But even he can't ignore these serendipitous signs from nature.

I'm sure if he could talk he'd agree.

But for now, I'm choosing to believe that these three emissaries are affirming that stem cell treatment will be giving him his wings back.

Testing, One, Two, Three

Our trip back from Arizona takes six hours, but time whizzed. Which is amazing since I drive with someone who doesn't talk much (understatement) and, mid desert, for at least two hours, there's no radio reception.

Time seems to speed up when I'm either scared to get someplace or excited about the outcome. Both happened on this short trip to see if Michael qualifies for the stem cell treatment study.

In January, while Michael was at the tail end of his rehab hospital stay, two friends simultaneously told me about a stem cell research study they read an article about. I knew nothing about stem cell therapy except it's supposed to be pretty amazing and, for whatever reason, is highly controversial.

Without hesitation, I contacted the sponsoring organization and was told that they were "really swamped" ever since the results were published about a famous athlete's miraculous

cure from a stroke after treatments.

The study coordinator asked a bunch of questions about

Michael – his history, information about his stroke, how much progress he had made, etc. I filled out all the forms, glanced briefly at the disclaimers and cautions, mailed over the requested doctor reports and waited to hear back.

Figuring they'd contact me in a month or so, but with everything else going on, it got filed in the back of my mind, underneath trying to figure out how we were going to survive.

When the dust settled after being discharged from the rehab hospital, I emailed the coordinator to check in. It took two weeks to hear back with a brief reply: "I will let you know as soon as possible but we are really busy."

Every two weeks or so I would email her, and each time it would take two weeks or more to hear back the same reply. This continued for six months.

The last time I heard from her was in May. Her response contained more of a commitment: "Michael should be getting into the study soon!"

Honestly, it never occurred to me that he *wouldn't* get in considering how positive the emails were (whenever I would receive one). I was more anxious than frustrated, and, considering this was a study (Read: free) I tiptoed on egg shells not wanting to be a nudge.

Figuring that, with everything else in such perfect Divine Order in my life, I didn't need to worry about this. *All in due time* was my mantra.

Fast forward to July.

We are staying at the healing resort, with forty hours of hyperbaric oxygen treatments under Michael's belt. Each time go here I get more involved helping write and design their websites, write press releases and do other marketing tasks. The owner talks openly about all aspects of the business and we are very chummy.

One afternoon while Michael's in the oxygen tank, my thoughts wander to the stem cell research study. What the heck, nothing to lose, so I decide to be more assertive about getting him   into the program.

In what could only be described as a backwards déjà vu, I flash on seeing two names at the bottom of the very first email I had received back in January. Bingo, I find it immediately.

I compose an email and send it off to the Other Name.

Honestly I'm tired of hearing he will be "getting in soon" since this person's definition of "soon" is clearly different than mine.

Prefacing the email with an apology for perhaps being pushy, and not wanting to step over any bounds, I explain the six months of fruitless correspondence. I boldly ask if there's anything she can do to expedite this for us. Within minutes after hitting send, I receive a very apologetic reply and an offer to call and discuss when Michael can come in!

Without waiting for the keyboard to cool off, I call her post haste.

Answering the same list of questions I'd been asked in January, the difference being six months of therapy without significant shifts. She seems oddly happy to hear that and immediately sets a date for us to come to Arizona to do an assessment.

Her final words are: "I'm sure Michael will be perfect for this study!"

My final words to her are "Thank you so much. You are truly a miracle!"

My next task is to figure out how to get there since I recently purchased an electric car. It can barely make it 60 miles between charges (don't believe the hype that they get 90 miles!). A dear friend offers to trade cars for a few days, instantly handling that concern.

Next: Where to stay for three days?

I remember that my cousin lives in Arizona, so, on a whim I text her. Ends up her house is approximately twenty minutes from the hospital where the testing will take place! She immediately insists that *mi casa es su casa.* Gratefully I accept the next miracle that's starting to overflow on my plate.

Our six hour drive consists of a new Michael quirk: Like an excited four year old on their very first road trip, he waves hi to every truck we drive by. Until he falls asleep for the rest of the drive.

Although it's only a few standard tests like an EKG and a CT scan and a neurological assessment, Michael's filled with apprehension. I couldn't be more excited.

The first person we meet is the Other Name study coordinator who replied to my somewhat pathetic email. When she introduces herself, spontaneously she grabs me and envelopes me with a big hug, apologizing again for her colleague's lack   of rapid response. Without stepping on anyone's toes, she reassures that she will take good care of us. Instant relief.

Directing through the very crowded neurology office, she ushers us directly into the exam room. The staff all knows her, treating her like royalty which, in my book she already is.

With less than a five minute wait, the doctor barrels in, clumsily crashing into Michael's wheelchair and almost doing a header. He reminds me of an older Doogie Houser: Thirty five at the most, navy blue tee shirt, faded jeans that fit snugly over a bit of a paunch, tousled sandy brown hair and cordially funny. If I had met him in other circumstances, I never would've pegged him as a "doctor type."

Asking the same litany of questions I now know by heart, he proceeds to direct Michael to follow various commands. "Move your arm," (still no movement), "Move your leg" (a little bit of movement).

He then rattles off a list of simple multiple choice questions for him to answer. Doctor pointing to his watch: "Michael, is this   a clock, a watch or a crayon?"

Michael, with full confidence clearly states "A crayon!" like duh, of course.

Doctor: "Are you sure it's a crayon?" He subtly tries to help. Is   it cheating if the doctor gives the correct answer?

Michael nods his head as he proudly repeats the word *crayon*   just to make sure we all heard his obviously accurate answer.

It's bizarre that he has such a difficult time with questions like that since I know he understands everything I say and comprehends exactly what's going on. Synapses are weird for sure.

A few more similar questions ensue with Michael unable to answer most of them. The doctor adds up his score and happily reports that Michael got a 13. Laughing, I tell him that 13 is my lucky number, but what does that score mean?

A 13 on any test sounds like a fail, but apparently failing is a good thing when it comes to qualifying for the stem cell study: *He qualifies!*

As we exit the doctor's office, our personal angel casually mentions that we are sure lucky to get into the study. "How many people are participating?" I ask. Her answer shocks me: "Three groups of 35 and this is the last group. And, Royce, there are only two spots left!"

I assumed there were hundreds, maybe even thousands, so to find out that there were only 105 total participants has me realize just how fortunate we are!

The first part of our drive home is spent emotionally explaining just how miraculous it is to be accepted in this study. Michael completely understands, and continues to wackily wave to every truck we pass. Until he falls asleep.

We are scheduled to go back for treatment on September 7th. One day infusing the stem cells, and nine days of observation. Then back every three months for a year of assessment. Lots of driving!

In my excitement, I don't ask many questions. Honestly, I don't care. All I know for sure is the heavens parted to get him into this study.

Our cup of miracles is runneth-ing over. What an honor it is to help this burgeoning field of scientific discovery and hopefully help a man who swears a watch is a crayon.

Stem Cell 101

It's Monday, September 6th, and Michael is clearly freaking about the stem cell infusion scheduled for the next day. He's trying to act cool, but his worried look gives him away.

In his pre-stroke days, we'd talk deeply about our fears, openly expressing even the most minute, illogical concerns to the other who would just listen, non-judgmentally. It's difficult for him to not be able to do that. I try to intuit what his fears could be and give voice to them so they can be released and not acted on.

People keep asking me for information about the stem cell study, how it works, where they infuse it, where do they get the cells from, etc., but honestly I have no idea. Kinda don't want   to know.

Just glad to be doing this.

It's one of those *on a wing and a prayer things*, wait to see what happens, try not to have any expectations, but hope that Michael has miraculous results. Since the entire Universe opened its arms for us to have this opportunity, there's gotta be huge reasons for it.

Keeping my fingers crossed for incredible shifts in his ability to talk and regain movement on his right side.

Simultaneously, hoping this doesn't end up some Big Spiritual Lesson about letting go of expectations.

Or something equally growth-full, please.'

There's a lot of discussion about expectations in my classes. The way I define them is: A fear-based *demand* for something *external* to make us happy, save us, bring us peace, fulfill us, make us feel loved, important, etc. Like a foot-stomping child at a toy store who simply MUST have that latest toy or he will just die.

Or when one simply MUST have one's husband back to how he was pre-stroke. Ahem.

We all have endless lists of expectations, each with specific itemized requirements. Of course, the Higher Truth is: *Nothing external can ever make us happy,* so it's a futile dance.

However, we are *completely convinced that eventually something will* make us happy even though it's *never worked yet!*

A 24/7 fantasy we live in!

Here's the "joke" about expectations: *If one of our needy demands happens to get fulfilled, we experience temporary happiness at best* because 1) it's probably not enough; 2) it's not exact to our specifications; or 3) it didn't arrive exactly how we thought it should.

"Well, those roses you gave me were nice but they were red and you know I love pink and you only sent a dozen and besides I had to ask for them so they don't count!"

Being willing to let go of expectations and trust the process of life as it unfolds, is an incredibly peaceful place to be, and is possibly one of our biggest challenges. One we are all here to accomplish whether we know it or not.

When we arrive at the hospital Tuesday morning at 7:00, they put Michael through the same litany of tests – urine, blood, cardiac, neuro. We settle into his room in the afternoon,   meet his nurse and the waiting begins.
As we numbly stare at the TV, my thoughts veer to all the expectations I have, even though I'm trying *really hard* not to.

The nurse keeps coming in to make sure we don't need anything, and on one of his entries he's loudly singing the Beatles song, "Let it be." I chuckle at the appropriateness.

The study coordinator texts every hour letting me know the infusion will happen "any time." The day drags on.

Apparently, it's a complicated process and takes quite a while to "prepare" cells for infusion. Seems like they're doing it one cell at a time.

At 5:00 one final text comes through saying she's on her way with the cells!

First they scratch in a tiny amount under his skin to make sure there's no allergic reaction. Wouldn't that be something after all this if he has an allergic reaction! T.G. he doesn't, so the infusion officially begins.

The nurse attaches the "infuser thing" (yes, that's what he keeps calling it!) to the line they've opened in Michael's arm. I watch mesmerized as a vial of cells destined to perform   miracles pours directly into a vein in his left arm.

In an hour, all those little guys are infused.

Now what?

We watch more TV, wait for the nurse to come in to take his vitals which the next shift continues to do. Every two hours.

All night long.

I somehow sleep through it even though laying on an uncomfortable vinyl couch.

When we get up the next morning, part of me starts observing Michael for even the slightest nuance of change.

None.

As the day goes on, I'm getting more and more irritated with him.

Snappy. Sarcastic. Impatient. All symptoms that something is going on inside me.

Could it be an expectation?

I become bitchier every minute. Michael, in his infinite wisdom (even without being able to use words), pulls me to his side and grunts *what' the hell is going on* in "clear" Neanderthal.

Busted.

Tearfully, I confess that, although I know that stem cells can't possibly have an effect in minutes, part of me is still hoping for that Instant Miracle. The one I've been holding my breath for these past nine months.

Phew. My bitchiness meter instantly drops to zero.

Six Days Later

Six days have passed since the stem cell infusion. Driving home in a blur of hopefulness equally mixed with *glad this is done.*

There haven't been any major changes of note. But I know there will be. Not from a fear-based, expectational place, but from a peaceful, intuitive sense.

I finally got the nerve up to ask the research director about the results they've been having from this study (I hadn't asked previously because I didn't want to have any expectations... ha!). She said that they've had great success with people who   had strokes like Michael's.

However, she did say that it will take a while.

I tried not to ask how long, but it popped out.

"From three months up to a year," she offered.

Can I do three months without having expectations? Hope so.

No expectations, of course.

November Changes?

Incredibly, it's been exactly one year since Michael's stroke. They say time flies when you're having fun, or as you get older, but no one tells you that it flies (with moments of airbrushed blurs) when your life is turned upside down.

We're sitting at the Thanksgiving table with several members of my surrogate family. The host poses the meaningful question to all gathered: *"What are you thankful for?"*

Without hesitation, I look over at my husband, still struggling daily to come all the way back.

Unlike Michael, who still isn't able to form many words, mine come easily: *"I'm thankful that Michael is here with me and that he continues to get better, even slightly, every single day."*

I'm still filled with trusting optimism as we go through this journey of healing. Admittedly, there are days we both want to give up, yet we choose to persevere. We know that, although this recovery process is slower than I ever thought it would be, IT IS happening.

Daily, we get inspired witnessing fellow stroke survivors at his outpatient rehab facility who persist, cheer leading us with hope. Repeatedly, they assure us that, even after far longer than a year, recovery does happen.

With work.

Every day is an interesting adventure. I'm able to see improvements just by comparing how he was even just a few months ago. I wish they were more dramatic, but I'm grateful for subtle.

As of yet no startling differences since September's stem cell infusion. However, he's able to do a few more things independently such as brushing his teeth and shaving.

Woohoo!

Still waiting in anticipation to see what happens. They say it can take months before those little buggers kick in.

Although his vocabulary still consists of maybe twenty words (the ones that pop out effortlessly are still those of the four letter variety, all used appropriately), he's completely present, understands everything that's said or requested of him without confusion.

That's a huge change.

Here's the highlight: Last week while watching TV, out of the blue he indicated wanting to play Scrabble! (Don't ask how I translated this request, but somehow I did!)

Pre-stroke Michael was a Scrabble maniac, at least six games going at any one time on his cell phone. It was rare anyone ever beat him, and even rarer to have him not put down at least one seven letter word per game. You know, those words that get 50 bonus points.

Not knowing what to expect, I dusted off my parents' old Scrabble board that I had inherited, handed him the letter bag and he carefully counted out seven. Graciously, I let him go first. Astoundingly, the first word Michael played was a seven letter one! Without my help!

Unlike the virtual board used now-a-days, I had to actually figure out the points. I added up his word points and wrote down 28. He started frantically pointing, saying *no, no!* Figuring I had added incorrectly, I re-did the math. Twenty eight again. *"NO!!!,"* he continued to insist even more vehemently.

Although he's always right when it comes to math, I insisted I was right this time. Somehow he got the message across that I'd forgotten to add those pesky 50 bonus points!

Freudian Slip, undoubtedly.

We played for over an hour. Although he needed my help now and then, basically he put together all his words and played one mean challenge. I ended up beating him (phew!) but it was a close game.

I'm amazed at this undeniable progress. This from a man who still can't retrieve the words to request ice tea, the drink he wants at least four times a day. The brain is a weird, complex organ for sure.

Although his official outpatient therapy is pretty much finished, I discovered all kinds of wonderful opportunities at Rancho to continue to participate in. When I heard they offered art classes, I asked if he wanted to attend and he reluctantly said yes. We agreed to give it a try.

Wasn't sure what how he'd react (would this be frustrating or a challenge to enjoy?), but from the minute he picked up a brush, his innate artistic talents started reemerging in amazing ways.

He didn't know what to paint, so the art volunteer handed him a National Geographic magazine to look through for inspiration. He located an aerial photograph of a landscape and started painting from it.

For two solid hours he focused on his creation, turning this realistic image into an abstract representation. The result was phenomenal; I was completely flabbergasted. Now, he's excited to attend every week, spending several hours creating paintings that are usually abstract, but meticulously thought out.

When we found out about painting classes being taught by a professional artist, he could hardly wait to sign up. By attending both classes, his abilities are blossoming and he's able to trust himself even more. He even sold several paintings and was given two commissions at the yearly art show at Rancho, a huge boost to his self-confidence.

Although this has been the most challenging of all times in my life, my virtual family reading these postings and offering loving, caring, supportive words, has been a true source of strength and inspiration.

I'm beyond thankful this Thanksgiving.

For Give

At a party, sitting among friends, Michael puts his hand on my arm. He looks straight at me, with a seriousness that rarely shadows his face.

"What's wrong?" I ask out of habit as well as an ongoing concern about his health that's still easily triggered.

The words I don't know I so desperately want to hear come easily: *"I forgive you."*

I sob in his arms. My friends look on, but no one asks what's going on. I'm glad.

"Thank you Michael. Thank you. Thank you."

I know now I can forgive myself. For this and all past lives we've shared.

Thank you.

One, Two, Cha Cha Cha

As we finish breakfast, suddenly Michael starts saying "Cha Cha."

Not having a clue as to why he would suddenly want to dance the Cha Cha, I ask him to repeat the words. "Cha Cha!" he says loudly, with more conviction and clarity.

Even though I'm probably wrong, I ask anyway: "Do you want to dance the cha cha cha?"

"No! Cha Cha!!" he insists.

Twenty minutes back and forth, getting nowhere.

"I'm sorry Michael but I have no idea what you mean. We need to leave to get to speech therapy. Hopefully Randy will be able to figure out what you mean."

Brush teeth, get dressed, put on jacket, out the door, into the car.

He starts up immediately, a tone of amazement that I can't determine what he is trying to get across: *"Cha Cha!"*

The entire hour drive consists of him saying those two words, until finally, in utter frustration, I tell him to stop.

"Michael, I can't do this anymore! I have no idea what you are trying to get across. I'm so sorry, but can we just drop it for now?"

Dejectedly, he does.

As we walk into Randy's office, I quickly relay the dilemma, throwing up my hands and saying "Okay, he's all yours! Figure it out!" and close the door behind me.

Twenty minutes later, I hear laughter from the therapist. The door flies open and, with a look of victory she says "I figured out what he's trying to say!"

"Oh my God, please tell me!"

"Well, you aren't going to believe this, but what he means to say is Zsa Zsa! Wasn't she an actress or a singer?"

This therapist is way too young to know anything about Zsa Zsa Gabor, so I tell her a bit about who she was.

"But why was Michael suddenly obsessing about her?"

The therapist takes me into her office.

"What day is today, Michael?" she asks with a twinkle in her eye.

"Cha Cha birthday!" he responds, as proud as if he had just discovered the cure for cancer.

"Holy shit!" I exclaim. "Zsa Zsa's birthday? How in the hell did you know that? And, more importantly, why did you know that?"

He shrugs his shoulder and begins to laugh.

All three of us have a good laugh, but one of us is befuddled as to why this random actress' birthday? I didn't even know he was a fan!

Will I ever understand how this man's brain works or how/why he knows it's Zsa Zsa's birthday?

I hope she's watching from wherever she landed and is having a good laugh as well.

Motions of Emotions

Whenever I ask Michael, *are you upset that (fill in the blank) happened?* He looks puzzled and says "No."

Either he's reached a state of Buddha-hood, or some part of his brain has switched off to anger as well
Recently, I decided a different tactic.

I'm constantly "encouraging" (aka kicking him in the butt) to get him to do things that I know will help his recovery. It's a constant battle, and to have my side win takes determination and grit.

And often treating him like a four year old.

Sometimes it works, and often it doesn't. We get into "fights" about this on a daily basis. Boy, it's hard to have a fight with someone who cannot use words. Somehow we manage.

When yet another squabble is about to occur today, (he refuses to move to a closer in a theater because he would have to transfer from his wheelchair, no big deal) I decide to do something different: I move to a better seat and leave him there by himself.

When the show is over, he doesn't even try to apologize. Usually, he gives me a puppy dog look and says "I'm sowee!" and that's supposed to fix everything. Well, it doesn't, and he knows it.

After the play, we drive home with both of us in silence. I've been silent ever since. Giving him the silent treatment.

How ironic.

Next morning I go to his bedside and gently wake him up.
"Michael, I just need to say how angry I was yesterday."
He looks at me with concern.

"In fact, I don't think I've ever been angrier. It felt like a slap
in the face that you wouldn't just move up a few rows so I
could see the performance better. There was no reason I
could figure that you wouldn't do that for me. Felt like you
just didn't care, and that really hurt."

Sad face but no words.

"So, what I realized was I just need to not ask, and just tell
you what to do. It goes against my nature, but I think your
stroke has affected you in ways I'm just starting to
understand. Even after all this time."

One of the strengths of our relationship was always making
decisions together. We'd talk it out until a mutual choice
could be found without either of us having to compromise.

We learned early on that if we couldn't agree , there was
always a reason. Eventually, when we'd discover what it was,
we would shake our heads and say, see, that's why we
couldn't agree. It made it easier the next time.

Since neither was the Alpha Dog in our marriage, it's difficult
to treat him like this. However, I need to keep reminding
myself that he's not who he used to be.

And, neither am I. We'll see how this works.

It's New Year's Eve, 2017. These past three years have brought   a slew of important spiritual life lessons, ones I apparently   needed to continue to fully grok.

One of my Top Five this life is learning patience. Yeah, managing that mysterious, seemingly endless time, when it seems like nothing is happening.

Like Michael's recovery.

Strokes take a helluva long time to "come back" from, and even though I thought Michael would be the exception, that hasn't happened. Although he's made progress, it's inches on a ten yard tape measure.

 Since I'm with him all the time, I don't see much improvement, but others do, which helps me trust that, yes, there's hope.

The hardest part is getting him to *care* about his recovery.

Pre-stroke Michael cared passionately about everything.

Recently, one of his therapists explained that his stroke affected his frontal lobe. This is the area that just happens to be in charge of motivation.

Explains a lot.

I know that if the Old Michael were looking at this New Michael, he'd be filled with disgust, desperately wanting to do anything possible to get better. Without prodding, he'd undoubtedly be religiously going to the gym, practicing his speech, flinging down his cane, and nothing would stop him. Since that part no longer exists, I've opted to become that for him.

I've gone back and forth about that since, on one hand, he's so content just as he is. However, I feel a commitment to his soul to do everything I can to wake up those synapses and help him back.

Looking at the images on his latest brain scan it's impossible to deny: A Grand Canyon size hole gapes back at us. Asking this neurologist whether there will be improvement, he states the usual company line: *Brains are plastic and able to form new pathways.*

Even though that space looks cavernous?

No answer.

But, I won't ever lose motivation no matter what any doctor says.

Sadly, no matter how many times I remind him that, the Old Michael would NEVER want to be the way he is now, my words bounce in that cavern, echoing back to me.

Which is really quite Zen-like in a way: *Acceptance of what is.*

Okay, I'm envious.

Back to my Big Lesson of patience . I've met dozens of stroke victims who remind me it takes years, decades even, and to never give up. Okay, got it: I will never give up.

In his own way, Michael reflects that to me. His jigsaw puzzle expertise has come back with a vengeance. Any time we're home, he spends hours on end putting together 1000 and 2000 piecers. He never needs a break, never gets frustrated. It's all he wants to do, actually.

I watch him in amazement as he sorts out piece by piece, patiently finding where they belong, never wanting to pull his hair out and run out of the room. Like I do.

And, when he's done, he just takes them apart and puts them in their box. Doesn't ever want to save any; it's all about the process.

His profound message?

Life is not the absence of challenges, but rather learning to slowly, courageously, gracefully, take the pieces you were given and figure out the enigma you've chosen this time.

Then, when it's all put together, feel pride but no attachment,   just take it apart and move to the next one.

Through my years of teaching others about trust, I've mostly mastered it for myself, but that limbo period is always the hardest. Watching my puzzle meister, he reminds me that it's those between-times when the most is happening – things are integrating, pieces are falling into place, others arrive in our   life, and we're being readied for our next leap.

Honestly, the longer the limbo, the bigger that leap will be.

We'll soon look back to where we were and understand why it needed to take as long as it took. "Divine Timing" is what I call   it.

There's incredible value in learning to wait in trust through transition times. It takes courage to sit in the mystery; to admit what no longer works without knowing what will; to not make rash decisions or give up out of frustration.

Evolution from one way of being to another can't be rushed. A new life can't be forced into existence.

Maybe it's about being in joy as you put together any puzzle you are solving.

Michael takes as long as he needs to put together his ridiculous puzzles. He will take as long as he needs to return completely.

Or not.

Sometimes life requires that we simply. Just. Wait. In. Courage. And. Trust.

And work tirelessly on whatever puzzle life hands us.

Break on Through

We started meeting with an outpatient Life Coach at Rancho. We're the first couple, as well as the first aphasic stroke survivor, she's ever worked with. Nice to be guinea pigs!

The first few meetings are mostly getting to know us, some testing, exploratory questions and figuring out the best way to help Michael communicate. Predictably, lots of spontaneous tears from The Wife. Even after three years, still so much sadness bubbles up.

Our coach is amazing. So caring and compassionate, yet very stick-to-the program professional. When all I need is to be heard, she gets it. When I'm in need of suggestions, she can tell, and happily share her expertise. She's not about giving comfort and sympathy, but rather, pragmatic solutions to day-to-day living with disability.

Having never experienced Life Coaching, I didn't know what to expect. Our coach explained that each session emphasizes creating measurable goals, then checking in the following week to see how they went.

On the surface, our goals appear small: Shaving by himself; showering by himself; drying his showered body by himself; cleaning his own glasses; taking the initiative to walk around the house without me reminding (read: bugging) him; walking at least 20 minutes a day.

To us, they were monumental.

Being the competitive person that he is, setting quantifiable goals is motivating. Each weekly report is glowing; our coach is thrilled.

Today's meeting is life-changing. Just when I think there can't be more sadness to let out, this brilliant coach is somehow able to crack open the door once again. Doesn't take much.

The session starts with me describing a free 15 minute 'intuitive life-reading' call I received last week.

"I never do things like this, but this person didn't seem like your typical psychic. I read her website and she's really higher consciousness. There was something about what she does that seemed like something I needed," I explain.

"Tell me what happened," she asks, sincerely curious.

"Well, I told her briefly about Michael and how frustrating it is that he has no motivation to get better. I told her how I constantly feel like a bitch having to push him so hard. It really goes against my nature and how our relationship used to be."

I continue: "Immediately, she tuned in energetically and started describing a past life. She tells me a little bit about it, but emphasizes that, in that life, I wasn't supported. I've remembered tons of past lives in the inner work I do, but I've never seen that one."

"Instead of going more into the details of that life, she honed in on the feeling I had about not being able to advocate for myself."

Telling our coach everything from this reading, I leave the most important detail until the end: "She told me that, because of not advocating for myself in that life, I've set up a situation where I need to advocate for my husband."

"She explained that I need to 'hold advocacy' for him, and to shift from seeing myself as The Bitch, trying to make him want to get better, into being his advocate."
Our coach listens intently.

"You know, there was something so incredibly powerful about just shifting how I perceive my role. It completely lightened up the entire situation. I feel so empowered by it!"

"Wow, that's great!" she says with amazement. Not sure she's had to deal with many clients bringing in psychic readings into their session, but she certainly didn't show any confusion. Or judgment.

"So, Michael, how do you feel about that?"

She makes sure to direct questions at Michael even though he's barely able to speak. She's able to "get" him without struggle or frustration.

"Okay," he shakes his head and replies.

She senses something else going on, so takes it further.

"Michael, is everything okay?"

He says yes, but she looks disbelieving.

"Michael, it just seems like there's something you're holding back."

He gets a morose look and lowers his head.

"Stroke..." he somehow finds the word.

"Three years...." he squeezes out.

"Yes, Michael, it's been three years since your stroke," I confirm.

His face is uncharacteristically solemn.

Even though I talk about it all the time, take him to therapy several times a week and he's had countless doctor's appointments, I'm not sure he knows what happened to him. This intuitive coach takes it further. She immediately hones in on what's going on. Far better than his wife ever could.

"Michael, are you sad about having a stroke?"
His head nods as he looks down at the ground.

"Are you afraid of letting Royce know how you are really feeling?"

Another head nodding, sad face.

"Why?" she prods, gently but firmly.

No reply.

A couple of other guesses and she nails it: "Are you trying to protect her?"

"Yes."

Tears start an uncontrollable downpour. Loud, insistent, gut-wrenching crying that neither our coach nor I anticipate. We don't even try to control our own tears.

This lasts for several minutes.

Once able, I get up and go over to him, wrapping my arms around him as we sob as one.

"You don't need to protect me, Michael," I say through my tears.

"It's okay to feel whatever you're feeling. It's important to let it out. Honestly, I think I've been feeling your sadness for both of us for a very long time."

Life coach observes quietly as we go through this together.

I've never felt more love tor this man who, all this time, has been trying to save me in the only way he could: By not letting on how truly sad he is.

Something inside shifts. Monumentally. Magically, I feel three years of sadness lift, knowing I don't have to feel it for both of us any longer. I can stop being the other side of the see-saw for my husband.

Right then, I also know I can stop being The Bitch.
Session is done. All three of us hug.

My ability to accept this Buddha-child combination exactly as he is grows. Time for both of us to completely step out of denial.

Floaty, I push his wheelchair to the car. Our connection feels like it used to. Two equals on the same path, loving and supporting each other, speaking the truth even when painful.

Even without many words.

Miraculous.

Epilogue

It's a difficult choice to end my writing here since there's no *happily ever after chapter*, no bragging finale *"and now Michael is back!"*

Although there's continuous, SLOW, progress, I'm as committed as ever to never give up. I'm told repeatedly that stroke victims can still improve even 20 years later. I see undeniable proof of that at his rehab hospital.

So we keep on keepin' on, even though every single day there's a part of me that wants to just give up. Am I in denial or trust? How long does one hold onto hope when "reality" shows otherwise? Choosing to not "buy into" so-called reality has always been my mantra. Why? I know there are limitless possibilities and infinite miracles.

And, when someone we haven't seen in a few months comments how far Michael has come, my hope gets re-ignited.

Simultaneously, I work on accepting The New Michael – this combination manchild and sage. Acceptance is my ongoing challenge since he just might be this way the rest of his life. Trying to be acceptant of my own process to get there.

Reading through the previous pages doing my final edit, I'm reminded as to how far he's actually come. From a drooling zombie, to being fully present; from grunting and snapping, to getting words out more readily; from not being able to stand without support, to walking up to twenty minutes (when I can get him to).

He still has no motivation to recover, so I continue to hold that commitment for him, reminding him what The Old Michael would've wanted. He's getting better at accepting that I will   never relinquish that role.

Swinging like a pendulum, from joy to frustration is less dramatic and has longer space between swings. Seeing this man who looks like the man I married, but bears almost no other resemblance, still saddens me, frequently.   But my tears   are less frequent.

Admittedly, I still catch myself occasionally pondering :
Would it have been easier had he died?   It's like being a widow, unable to justify mourning since he's still technically here. My pondering doesn't last long because every second of each day I'm grateful he is still here.

Although he's my most challenging Life Teacher, he also brings more joy to my life than anything.

Yes, the Michael I married is in there. Whenever he pokes his head out even slightly, hopefulness flickers. But, soon, he slinks back into his world of silence, with no impetus to return.

Because, he truly doesn't care.

So, dear reader, may these words remind you, in any time of transition: May you learn trust during your limbo of uncertainty; may you gift yourself with whatever helps you brave forward during dark times; and may you be open to receive clarity during times of confusion, doubt or loss.

Remember: *We are spirits on an amazing adventure in this physical realm, trying to recollect who we truly are moment-to-moment with each experience furthering our abilities to love ourselves so we can truly love others.*

And, we are all doing this together.

May you soar gracefully; trust all of life's leaps, growing wings   on the way down.   My own wings continue to grow stronger each day.

Epilog Deux: Written by a Friend.

Sometimes I imagine you and Michael, after you've both "transitioned," between lives, reminiscing about this lifetime.

Michael: "So...what did you think about me doing that whole 'stroke thing?'"

Royce: "That was so unexpected. I never saw that one coming!"

Michael: "Yeah, thought that one was pretty ingenious. Really rocked your boat!"

Royce: "Boy, did it ever!"

Michael: "I always said I would be there to support you in that lifetime – whatever it took. I wanted to keep my commitment to you."

Royce: (tearful) "I am so grateful you did. I got to step out of my life, so to speak, and see how much I really, really love you   It was so healing! And I got to write and write and write...that was so joyful. Then, all that transpired after that was just the   juiciest, wildest, miraculous adventure I've ever experienced!   And I thought that lifetime was just going to be   so difficult and hopeless. I wanted so much to give up, but I stubbornly refused to do THAT again. So glad I held on long enough to get to the best part!!!"

Michael: "Me too. So, wanna go do another life adventure?"

Royce: "Okay – but I still haven't decided whether I want to be famous rock star or something else. There are so many possibilities!"

Michael: "Wait....don't you have to go back to our planet of origin? You promised them, after all."

Royce: "Well, after they saw how this planet transformed from my teachings, they gave me a pardon and said I was released from that obligation. But I would like my family from that planet join us this time around on earth."

Michael: "Fantastic! So, this time I decided I wanna be a famous baseball pitcher. How about we meet when you come sing the National Anthem at the opening ceremony, if they still do that kind of stuff. You'll do it with such soul! I'll be so taken with you. And you'll think I'm just the most handsome, charming guy you've ever met."

Royce: "Oh Michael, you're so darn romantic....and funny! Will that mean I have to like baseball?

Michael: "You better!"

Royce: "Well, we'll see about that! So, let's figure out how we'll connect with those other people we love so much...gotta keep the team together!"

Michael: "Not to worry. They'll find us. Or we'll find them."

Royce: "Of course. They always have!"

ROYCE MORALES

Royce Morales is the developer of **Perfect Life Awakening**, a spiritually based, experiential, "inner-makeover" seminar series that creates profound personal transformation. For over three decades, she's been offering her empowering techniques to thousands, accelerating self-discovery and growth in an intimate group setting.

She devised a potent, inner-processing technique that helps uncover and resolve subconscious, fear-based 'programming.' Her work gets to the root of what's preventing a life of joy, love and purposefulness.

Royce is the author of *Know: A spiritual wake-up call*, a detailed explanation of her teachings. Written in a hands-on way, this book is designed as a tool to help the reader experience inner transformation.

She also authored *Want: True love, past lives and other complications*, a fictionalized story of what soulmate love really is, sprinkled generously with her teachings.

Along with her husband Michael, she created **Harmony Works**, a trailblazing, eco-conscious, hand-craft shop and gallery in Redondo Beach. This spiritually-themed, soul-nurturing venue was open for 21 years.

Royce is a contributing writer for various publications, a freelance creative and copy writer, web designer and ghost blogger for independent small businesses.

You can reach her or purchase books via her website: www.contentintentcopy.com

Made in the USA
Las Vegas, NV
04 December 2020